# The Tourism Issue

## ISSUES

### Volume 33

Editor

Craig Donnellan

*Independence*

Educational Publishers
Cambridge

First published by Independence
PO Box 295
Cambridge CB1 3XP
England

**British Library Cataloguing in Publication Data**
The Tourism Issue – (Issues Series)
I. Donnellan, Craig II. Series
338.4'791

ISBN 1 86168 216 6

**Printed in Great Britain**
MWL Print Group Ltd

**Typeset by**
Claire Boyd

**Cover**
The illustration on the front cover is by
Pumpkin House.

# CONTENTS

## Chapter One: The Tourism Industry

## Chapter Two: Responsible Tourism

# Introduction

*The Tourism Issue* is the thirty-third volume in the **Issues** series. The aim of this series is to offer up-to-date information about important issues in our world.

*The Tourism Issue* examines the tourism industry and the issue of responsible tourism.

The information comes from a wide variety of sources and includes:
Government reports and statistics
Newspaper reports and features
Magazine articles and surveys
Literature from lobby groups
and charitable organisations.

It is hoped that, as you read about the many aspects of the issues explored in this book, you will critically evaluate the information presented. It is important that you decide whether you are being presented with facts or opinions. Does the writer give a biased or an unbiased report? If an opinion is being expressed, do you agree with the writer?

*The Tourism Issue* offers a useful starting-point for those who need convenient access to information about the many issues involved. However, it is only a starting-point. At the back of the book is a list of organisations which you may want to contact for further information.

\*\*\*\*\*

# Global tourism: growing fast

## Information from People & the Planet

**B**y some measure tourism may already be the world's largest industry, with annual revenue approaching $500 billion. And it is growing fast, with airline arrivals expected to double by 2010.

Leisure is estimated to account for 75 per cent of all international travel. The World Tourism Organisation (WTO) estimated there were 698 million international tourist arrivals in 2000. They are expected to reach 1.6 billion in 2020. Domestic tourism (people going on holiday in their own country) is generally thought to be 4-5 times greater than international arrivals. The WTO puts global revenue from tourism in 2000 at US$476 billion.

The World Travel and Tourism Council (WTTC) predicts global turnover from tourism in 2001 will be around £2.3 trillion – 10.8 per cent of global GDP.

Globally, tourism accounts for roughly 35 per cent of exports of services and over 8 per cent of exports of goods (WTO). In 1995, 11 per cent of the global workforce – over 200 million people (predicted to rise to 340 million by 2005) – were directly or indirectly employed in tourism (International Labour Organisation – ILO).

These figures would make tourism the world's largest employer and arguable its largest business in terms of income.

- For 83 per cent of countries in the world, tourism is one of the top five sources of foreign exchange.
- Caribbean countries derive half their GDP from tourism (World Resources Institute).
- Benidorm's tourism industry accounts for 1 per cent of Spain's GDP.

### Where tourists go

Three-quarters of all international travellers visit a country in either Europe or North America. However, the share of international tourists travelling to Asia and the Pacific rose from just 1 per cent in 1950 to 16 per cent in 2000. By 2020, Asia will be the most popular destination after Europe, attracting a quarter of world tourist traffic. China is expected to unseat France as the most visited country and to become the fourth largest source of tourists.

### Where tourists come from

Over 80 per cent of international tourists come from just 20 countries in the North – 17 in Europe plus the USA, Canada and Japan. Five nations (the US, Japan, Germany, France and the UK) account for almost half of all tourist spending. Around 15 per cent of tourists

## World's top 15 tourism destinations

| Rank | International tourist Arrivals (million) | | % change 2000/1999 | Market share (%) 2000 |
|---|---|---|---|---|
| | 1999 | 2000 | | |
| 1. France | 73.0 | 75.5 | 3.4 | 10.8 |
| 2. United States | 48.5 | 50.9 | 4.9 | 7.3 |
| 3. Spain | 46.8 | 48.2 | 3.0 | 6.9 |
| 4. Italy | 36.5 | 41.2 | 12.8 | 5.9 |
| 5. China | 27.0 | 31.2 | 15.5 | 4.5 |
| 6. United Kingdom | 25.4 | 25.2 | -0.8 | 3.6 |
| 7. Russian Federation | 18.5 | 21.2 | 14.5 | 3.0 |
| 8. Mexico | 19.0 | 20.6 | 8.4 | 3.0 |
| 9. Canada | 19.5 | 20.4 | 4.9 | 2.9 |
| 10. Germany | 17.1 | 19.0 | 10.9 | 2.7 |
| 11. Austria | 17.5 | 18.0 | 2.9 | 2.6 |
| 12. Poland | 18.0 | 17.4 | -3.1 | 2.5 |
| 13. Hungary | 14.4 | 15.6 | 8.1 | 2.2 |
| 14. Hong Kong (China) | 11.3 | 13.1 | 15.3 | 1.9 |
| 15. Greece | 12.2 | 12.5 | 2.8 | 1.8 |

Data collected through August 2001

*Source: World Tourism Organization (WTO)*

originate in East Asia and the Pacific and 5 per cent in Africa, the Middle East, and South Asia combined.

## Industry organisations

- World Travel and Tourism Council (WTTC): A trade association based in Brussels and London and made up of around 70 chief executives of major airlines, hotel chains, cruise lines and catering companies.
- World Tourism Organisation (WTO): Based in Madrid and created by the United Nations, the WTO consists of a mix of 130-plus governments and 350 affiliated private enterprises. Compiles industry statistics and market trends.
- American Society of Travel Agents (ASTA): The largest travel trade association in the world, representing 26,500 travel agents in 170 countries (Honey).
- Association of British Travel Agents (ABTA): The trade association of the major British tour operators.

## Growth of tourism

International tourist arrivals increased from 25 million in 1950 to 698 million in 2000, and are predicted to grow to 1.56 billion by 2020 (WTO). Globally, the tourism industry is growing at 4.6 per cent (WTTC). The number of air passengers rose from 9 million in 1945 to 88 million in 1972, 344 million in 1994 and 1.6 billion in 1999, and is expected to double again by 2010. (International Civil Aviation Organisation: *In Focus*, Autumn 2000).

## Factors in tourism's growth include:

- Increasing leisure time: In 1936, the International Labour Organisation convention provided for one week's leave per year for workers in developed countries. In 1970, this was expanded to three weeks, and in 1999 to four weeks.
- Increased disposable income: Spending on leisure in the UK has risen from 9 per cent of household income in 1978 to 17 per cent in 1998 (Tearfund:

### The air industry

The air transport industry generates 24 million jobs and a gross annual output of US$1,140 billion a year (WTO). In 1999, there were 1.6 billion flights taken. There are roughly 1,200 airlines worldwide, of which around 300 fly internationally (OECD, 1997). Most major international airlines are now linked into four global 'alliances':

| Airlines | | | | |
| --- | --- | --- | --- | --- |
| Top 5 airlines (1996) | Revenue (US$bn) | Passengers (million) | Employees | Aircraft |
| American Airlines | 17.8 | 81.2 | 111,300 | 649 |
| United Airlines | 16.4 | 81.9 | 85,900 | 564 |
| Japan Airlines | 13.9 | 30.2 | 19,000 | 130 |
| Lufthansa | 13.8 | 41.4 | 57,999 | 314 |
| British Airways | 13.2 | 33.3 | 58,210 | 256 |

Source: Airline Business, 1997

*Tourism: An Ethical Issue*, 2000). In 1998-99, the UK Family Expenditure Survey found UK households spent £936 a year on holidays: 4.5 times more in real terms than 30 years previously.

- Falling real cost of air travel: Between 1978 and 1998, the real cost of air travel fell by 35 per cent (Air Travel Association). A thousand miles of air travel now requires 61 hours less work than it did a generation ago.

## Growth of tourism to the South

In 1950, 97 per cent of international tourists went to Europe or North America (in fact, to just 15 countries). By 1999 this had fallen to around 75 per cent. In the mid-1970s, 8 per cent of all international tourists were from the North visiting the South. By the mid-1990s, this had risen to 20 per cent (Honey). In 1999, more than 70 countries received over a million international tourist arrivals.

## Growth of tourism in/ from the South

In recent years, domestic and intra-

---

*International tourist arrivals increased from 25 million in 1950 to 698 million in 2000, and are predicted to grow*

---

regional tourism in the South has grown rapidly, especially in emerging economies such as Thailand, India, Korea, China and Mexico.

- Tourists originating in East Asia and the Pacific increased from 32.4 million in 1985 (9.9 per cent of world total) to 92.9 million in 1998 (14.6 per cent of world total).
- In 1995, 108 million people worked in tourism in China and South Asia, compared to only 42 million in the North (North America, Australasia, Japan and the European Community).
- Intra-regional tourism (people travelling within the same continent/region) accounted for 73 per cent of total tourist arrivals in East Asia and the Pacific in 1998. In Africa, intra-regional tourism increased from 38 per cent of all arrivals in 1980 to 60 per cent in 1990 (WTO).
- 90 per cent of visitors to national parks in Thailand, India and South Africa are domestic tourists (Ceballos-Lascurain 1996). Of 200,000 annual visitors to Kinabalu National Park in Sabah, Malaysia, 90 per cent are Malaysian. At Mt Bromo in Java, Indonesia, 70 per cent of visitors are Indonesian.

- The above article appeared in *People & the Planet* in May 2002. See their web site: www.peopleandplanet.net for further information.

© *People & the Planet 2000 – 2002*

# ABTA'S
# holiday trends

By *Sean Tipton*

## General travel trends for 2002 and beyond

### Cruising

Following a 10 per cent increase in numbers in 2000, cruising is set to further increase. Britain is now the second largest cruise market in the world, second only to the United States. The Caribbean and the Mediterranean are firm favourites for those flying to their holiday destination to join their cruise, fly-cruises to Scandinavia and Alaska look set to become increasingly popular. River cruising in Europe allowing the opportunity to travel from city to city and leisurely view the scenery, appeals to the more mature market. Many choose a two-centre holiday, combining a week on land with a week cruising and relaxing. September 11 has already discouraged many Americans from travelling abroad and this may well result in bargains for the UK market as cruise lines look to fill their berths.

### Long-haul holidays

ABTA/MORI research conducted in October 2000 asked 'If money were no object, where would you like to visit on holiday?' An overwhelming 22 per cent responded with Australia and 11 per cent with the United States. Clearly long-haul travel is still the dream for many.

The number of long-haul destinations on offer is increasing each year. The most popular is still Florida but numbers to Mexico have risen dramatically in recent years, reflecting the increased choice in charter flights, competitive prices and the British holidaymaker taking advantage of good value all-inclusive resorts.

The Far East is popular, not only with independent travellers, but also with those on inclusive tours. Thailand is a favourite with British holidaymakers, as are Malaysia, Singapore and, increasingly, Vietnam. India has a firm following and Kenya continues to attract those looking for a safari experience. South Africa is proving popular as a summer sun destination and the Emirates are attracting more visitors from Britain. Dubai has become a particular favourite for those looking for fine beaches and duty-free shopping.

A total eclipse on 4 December 2002 promises to be a big attraction for Australia and South Africa.

### Short breaks

More than 3.3 million people took a short break in 2001 (a figure that has been increasing steadily since 1990) and an increase in numbers is predicted again for 2002. With a significant increase in the numbers of airlines who offer short-haul, non-flexible (but very cheap) flights to European cities, we are likely to see the continued growth of short breaks. Most of these trips will be in addition to longer summer or winter holidays.

Dublin, Paris, Amsterdam and Rome are among the most popular cities but increasingly destinations such as Warsaw, Prague and other Eastern European cities are finding favour. Long-haul short breaks are also popular, with New York, Boston and Toronto all featuring as easy getaways and shopping weekends.

### Winter holidays

Snowsports play a vital part in the winter holiday market. Around 1.5 million people take a skiing holiday each year, many now opting to try snowboarding as well. The most popular destinations for skiing are France, Austria and Italy. Many people are choosing to travel further afield taking advantage of the strong pound and availability of charter flights, Canada and the United States have seen a massive rise in popularity over the past 10 years.

The winter sun market centres on the Southern Hemisphere. Tenerife and the other Canary Islands are the short-haul choice, with the Caribbean, Florida, Mexico, Australia and South Africa all offering an affordable winter sun experience.

### Low-cost airlines

The spectacular growth of the low-cost airlines in the last few years looks set to continue in 2002. They were one of the few sectors of the aviation industry to buck the trend following September 11 with most repeating an increase in numbers of up to 30% on 2000. With flights often being cheaper than a train ticket in the UK a weekend break in Europe has become a very enticing prospect rather than a luxury item. Cities such as Bologna and Naples in Italy, Copenhagen in Denmark, Zurich in Switzerland, Bordeaux and Lyon in France and Berlin in Germany are all on offer and the range is expanding.

• The above information is from the Association of British Travel Agents' (ABTA) web site which can be found at www.abta.com Alternatively, see page 41 for their address details.

# Facts and key issues

## Information from WWF-UK

### Facts

- Tourism is the largest and fastest-growing industry in the world.
- In 2000, there were nearly 700 million tourists, and in 2020, there will be around 1.6 billion.
- In 2000, across the global economy, travel and tourism accounted for around 11 per cent of world exports, goods and services, surpassing trade in food, textiles, and chemicals.
- Around 15 million people from the UK go on package holidays every year. That's roughly 30 holidaymakers jetting off every minute of every day.
- Around 3.5 per cent of greenhouse gas emissions come from air travel, a share that is expected to increase as air travel does.
- The Mediterranean is the world's most popular holiday destination, and more than 11 million British people visit the region every year.
- In the Mediterranean, tourism development is the single biggest threat to remaining areas of pristine coastline.
- Each year, around 5,000 hectares – an area about half the size of Paris – are cleared for golf courses, each of which can consume more than 2.3 million litres of water every day.
- Nearly 80 per cent of international tourists come from Europe and the Americas, while only 15 per cent come from East Asia and the Pacific, and five per cent from Africa, the Middle East and South Asia.
- Sometimes, as little as 10 per cent of the money spent on a holiday remains in the destination economy.
- In the UK, 80 per cent of all holidaymakers are carried by four big tour operators.
- Holidays involving air travel can probably never be wholly sustainable

### Key issues

- Tourism often occurs in areas that are rich in wildlife, such as coastal regions.
- Tourism can generate money for countries, people and conservation, but it can also divide communities and destroy fragile habitats such as reefs and coasts.
- Often only a small percentage of the money that a tourist spends on a holiday remains in the destination economy or benefits local people and business. This phenomenon is known as 'leakage'.
- Although around 80 per cent of UK package holidaymakers believe that it is important that their holidays do not damage the environment, they are ultimately motivated by cost when choosing a holiday.
- Health and safety are primary considerations for tour operators and their customers alike, but 'responsible tourism' requires that the well-being of the environment and local people have equal importance in a quality product.

• The above information is from WWF's web site which can be found at www.wwf.org.uk Alternatively see page 41 for their address details.

*© WWF-UK*

# The business of travel

## The nature of the tourist industry

Tourism is all about making a profit from our age-old desire to travel. Out modern global tourist industry speaks to other desires as well: to escape from the daily grind; to do something different; or to get the best deal for the cheapest price. Open any holiday brochure and you will see how well tour companies understand us!

The sheer scale of modern tourism means it touches not just those millions of us who can now afford to travel for pleasure; not just those who make a mint – or a pittance – from tourism; but also those who live in the places where we go on holiday. Nowadays, tourism reaches into every country in the world, even those afflicted by war or natural disaster.

The factors behind this huge growth are the modern technology which streamlines the messy business of international travel, and sophisticated marketing techniques which tempt us further and further away on holiday. Travel has never before been so fashionable and so affordable.

We are not individual travellers making our own arrangements at each step of the way. Even those of us who enjoy travelling independently make use at some point of services managed on a large scale. So whether we see ourselves as visitors, tourists or travellers, we are all taking advantage of a mass production process, organised by the travel and tourism industry.

How does this massive industry work? Think of it like any manufacturing industry: holiday destinations and their inhabitants are its raw materials; tourists and travellers are the consumers of its products – made by processing the raw materials and mixing them with imported components; tour operators and travel agents are its wholesalers and retailers, responsible for packaging and selling the products.

Like a car, holidays can be complex to create. The components of an average holiday are supplied by a range of interconnected businesses. At one end are small family-run enterprises offering specialist services such as transport, accommodation or entertainment to individual clients. At the other are multi-national companies, including famous British names such as Thomson and Airtours, aiming to control every aspect of package holidays, from the airlines, hotels and excursions to the agency used to book them. They decide which hotels will feature in their brochures and they fix prices with the hotel management and transport providers.

While there are some highly successful international tourism chains based in developing countries – hotel chains such as the Taj and

---

*Holiday destinations and their inhabitants are its raw materials; tourists and travellers are the consumers of its products*

---

Oberoi groups from India, for example – most head offices are based in the industrialised world.

Millions also travel on business, often taking the chance to add on leisure time. Many of tourism's facilities have to meet the tough standards of companies who require their employees to be disrupted as little as possible by the new environment they've come to work in .

If this is an industry churning out similar models for cost efficiency, it's also one that sees standardisation as a perfect goal in many cases. Once one hotel offers a swimming pool and golf course for stressed-out executives, the rest have to follow, whatever the local climate and living conditions. This drive for uniformity also tunes into the general desire for 'safe adventure'. Anything too different from what clients are used to may be commercially risky, although demand for something different and 'real' is growing, and has the potential to place a higher value on cultural diversity.

So, cost efficient, often standardised and ready to please the client at all costs – that's our modern mainstream tourist industry. And it's controlled for the most part, not by the countries who receive the tourists, but by those who send them.

### What a holiday costs

For a two-week holiday in Kenya a tourist spent:

    7% before the holiday
    83% to the tour operator
      – 10% travel agent
      – 40% flight
      – 40% accommodation
      – 10% local operators
    10% during the holiday

• The above information is an extract from *A Tearfund guide to Tourism – Don't forget your ethics!* produced by Tearfund. See page 41 for their address details.

© *Tearfund*

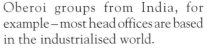

# Tourism highlights

## Information from the World Tourism Organization (WTO)

- Spurred on by a strong global economy and special events held to commemorate the new millennium, world tourism grew by an estimated 7.4 per cent in 2000 – its highest growth rate in nearly a decade and almost double the increase of 1999.

- According to results received by WTO through August 2001 the total number of international arrivals reached a record 699 million in 2000. In other words, nearly 50 million more arrivals were recorded, the same number of new tourists as a major destination such as Spain or the United States receives in the entire year.

- Europe – which accounts for 58 per cent of international tourism – grew by an impressive 6.1 per cent to 403 million arrivals, nearly 25 million more trips than one year earlier.

- All regions of the world hosted more tourists in 2000, although the fastest developing region continued to be East Asia and the Pacific with a growth rate of 14.7 per cent and some 14 million more tourists than 1999.

- Receipts from international tourism climbed to US$476 billion in 2000, an increase of 4.5 per cent over the previous year. Worldwide the average receipt per arrival amounted to US$680.

- Expectations for 2001 are for a more moderate pace of growth. Given the cooler economic climate it would be a good result if the tourism sector could consolidate the record growth of 2000 and add a modest increase.

## International tourist arrivals

Europe and the Americas are the main tourist-receiving regions. But since other regions are growing at a faster pace, their respective shares in the world total show a declining tendency. In 2000 Europe accounted for 58 per cent and the Americas for 18 per cent. East Asia and the Pacific is the region which has most benefited from this transformation of the market. Historical data show that this region experienced the highest growth rate, having obtained a 16 per cent share of the world market in 2000.

## International tourism receipts

In 2000, the receipts registered for international tourism amounted to over US$1 billion per year in 59 countries and territories out of approximately 200. The United States is the unchallenged leader with US$85 billion in international tourism receipts. Three important Mediterranean destinations – Spain, France and Italy – made around US$30 billion each. The United Kingdom registered US$20 billion and Germany, China, Austria and Canada earned over US$10 billion each.

## Regional results

### Africa

Africa increased its international arrivals by an estimated 4.4 per cent in 2000. While Zambia, Algeria, Mauritius, Morocco, Nigeria and Tunisia all enjoyed strong growth, two of Africa's biggest destinations stagnated or suffered – South Africa and Zimbabwe.

### Americas

Americas recorded its fastest growth in the Caribbean (7.5%), while North and Central America also showed solid increases, of 5.7 per cent and 7 per cent respectively. Despite the strength of the US dollar, international arrivals to the United States were up by 4.9 per cent due to continuing growth from major overseas markets.

---

*Receipts from international tourism climbed to US$476 billion in 2000, an increase of 4.5 per cent over the previous year*

---

### East Asia and the Pacific

East Asia/Pacific saw growth in tourist arrivals that was driven by big increases in China and its special administrative regions of Hong Kong and Macao. South-east Asia – especially Thailand, Malaysia, Cambodia and Vietnam – is becoming one of the world's favourite tourism destinations with demand outstripping tourist facilities. Australia enjoyed its own tourism boom due to the Sydney Olympics and surrounding publicity.

### Europe

Regional Europe was the star performer of world tourism in 2000, with tourists attracted to Germany for Expo 2000 and to Italy for the Vatican Jubilee. Eastern European countries recovered following the war in Kosovo and Turkey recuperated after two years of declining tourism due to instability and natural disasters.

### Middle East

Middle East tourism was set for its best year ever as tourists flocked to historic sites associated with the life of Jesus Christ on the 2000th anniversary of his birth. In the first nine months of the year, arrivals were up by as much as 20 per cent, but the region ended the year with a lower – yet vigorous – growth rate of 13 per cent due to the renewed violence in the last quarter of the year. The ongoing strong growth of Egypt is another substantial factor in the region's expansion.

### South Asia

South Asia is another of the success stories of 2000, with tourist arrivals growing by 11 per cent – nearly four points above the world average. Although it did not host any world-renowned events, tourists are increasingly seeking out its exotic destinations – especially Iran and India.

## International tourism expenditure

In 2000, 46 countries recorded more than US$1 billion in international tourism expenditure, with the big industrial economies clearly in the lead. The United States, Germany, the United Kingdom and Japan top the list with spending ranging from US$31 billion to US$65 billion per year. These four countries represent over one-third of total international tourism expenditure. They are followed by France, Italy, Canada, and the Netherlands. Each of these countries spends between US$12 and 17 billion, adding up to 12 per cent of total international tourism expenditure.

## Short-term prospects

The tourism sector in the upcoming year is not expected to perform quite as well as the event-filled year of 2000. The world economy was also remarkably strong in 2000, with world economic output as measured in Gross Domestic Product (GDP) growing by an extraordinary rate of almost 5 per cent. As a result disposable income increased and boosted discretionary spending on tourism. However, growth rates reached in 2000 for both tourism and economic output are not sustainable in the longer run and should be considered as exceptions.

For the tourism sector it would be a good result to consolidate the growth of the year 2000 and to increase by a more modest rate in the upcoming year. Initially, for 2001 a growth rate is anticipated around or somewhat below the 4.1 per cent average annual growth rate that is projected in WTO's long-term forecast *Tourism 2020 Vision* for the period up to 2020.

## Tourism 2020 Vision

*Tourism 2020 Vision* is the World Tourism Organization's long-term forecast and assessment of the development of tourism up to the first 20 years of the new millennium. An essential outcome of the *Tourism 2020 Vision* are quantitative forecasts covering a 25-year period, with 1995 as base year and forecasts for 2000, 2010 and 2020.

WTO's *Tourism 2020 Vision*

forecasts that international arrivals are expected to reach over 1.56 billion by the year 2020. Of these worldwide arrivals in 2020, 1.18 billion will be intraregional and 377 million will be long-haul travellers.

The total tourist arrivals by region shows that by 2020 the top three receiving regions will be Europe (717 million tourists), East Asia and the Pacific (397 million) and Americas (282 million), followed by Africa, the Middle East and South Asia.

East Asia and the Pacific, South Asia, the Middle East and Africa are forecasted to record growth at rates of over 5 per cent per year, compared to the world average of 4.1 per cent. The more mature regions Europe and Americas are anticipated to show lower than average growth rates.

Europe will maintain the highest share of world arrivals, although there will be a decline from 60 per cent in 1995 to 46 per cent in 2020. By 2010 the Americas will lose its number two position to the East Asia and the Pacific region which will receive 25 per cent of world arrivals in 2020 with the Americas decreasing from 19 per cent in 1995 to 18 per cent in 2020.

Long-haul travel worldwide will grow faster, at 5.4 per cent per year over the period 1995-2020, than intraregional travel, at 3.8 per cent. Consequently the ratio between intraregional and long-haul travel will shift from around 82:18 in 1995 to close to 76:24 in 2020.

• The World Tourism Organization is the only intergovernmental organisation that serves as a global forum for tourism policy and issues. Its Members include 139 countries and territories as well as over 350 Affiliate Members from the public and private sectors. WTO's mission is to promote and develop tourism as a significant means of fostering international peace and understanding, economic development and international trade. Visit their web site at www. world-tourism.org

© *World Tourism Organization(WTO)*

## World's top 15 tourism earners

| Rank | | International tourism receipts (US$ billion) | | % change 2000/1999 | Market share % 2000 |
|---|---|---|---|---|---|
| | | 1999 | 2000 | | |
| 1 | United States | 74.9 | 85.2 | 13.7 | 17.9 |
| 2 | Spain | 32.4 | 31.0 | -4.3 | 6.5 |
| 3 | France | 31.5 | 29.9 | -5.1 | 6.3 |
| 4 | Italy | 28.4 | 27.4 | -3.2 | 5.8 |
| 5 | United Kingdom | 20.2 | 19.5 | -3.4 | 4.1 |
| 6 | Germany | 16.7 | 17.8 | 6.5 | 3.7 |
| 7 | China | 14.1 | 16.2 | 15.1 | 3.4 |
| 8 | Austria | 12.5 | 11.4 | -8.7 | 2.4 |
| 9 | Canada | 10.2 | 10.8 | 5.9 | 2.3 |
| 10 | Greece | 8.8 | 9.2 | 5.0 | 1.9 |
| 11 | Australia | 8.0 | 8.4 | 5.3 | 1.8 |
| 12 | Mexico | 7.2 | 8.3 | 14.8 | 1.7 |
| 13 | Hong Kong (China) | 7.2 | 7.9 | 9.4 | 1.7 |
| 14 | Turkey | 5.2 | 7.6 | 46.8 | 1.6 |
| 15 | Russian Federation | 7.5 | – | | |

Data collected through August 2001      Source: World Tourism Organization (WTO)

# Could 'customised' trips be the death of the package holiday?

Thomson is to start charging for in-flight meals, hotel transfers and extra leg-room in a move that could spell the end of the package holiday.

The travel company says the extra charges will allow travellers more flexibility to create their own break in the sun.

But consumer groups fear it could be a ruse to introduce price rises and warn that families may rebel. Thomson insists the change is not being introduced to cover a surreptitious price increase – but it will be difficult for travellers to make sure.

The price of a 'no-frills' basic holiday should now appear cheaper in Thomson's Summer 2003 brochures, which will reach travel agents next week.

That should help to get customers signing on the dotted line, but the final price paid is likely to be very different from the brochure figure.

For a family of four who prefer to travel in relative comfort, rather than cattle class, and want a decent view, the difference could be well over £200.

In-flight meals will now be charged at £10 for adults and £5 for children, while extra leg-room in a premium cabin will start at £25 a seat.

There will be a minimum £25 charge for a taxi transfer from the airport to your hotel or apartment, and either £5 or £10 per person for a coach ride.

There will also be extra charges for those who want other 'frills' such as a balcony or a sea view.

Last year one firm even charged £15 per person to use a swimming pool, although Thomson has not gone that far.

In another major development, the UK's biggest package holiday company, Airtours – now MyTravel – is set to launch a no-frills, low-cost airline.

*By Sean Poulter, Consumer Affairs Correspondent*

The company is reacting to the success of budget carriers such as Easy-Jet and Go who have won over large numbers of travellers heading for hot spot destinations.

Their customers travel cheaply and book accommodation separately.

Thomson Holidays managing director, Chris Mottershead, said: 'Shoppers today appreciate choice.

'You don't just buy a coffee these days, you buy a latte, espresso or cappuccino.

> *'People will customise the holiday to suit their needs and they won't pay for anything they don't use'*

'It's the same with cars or new homes and we believe the same applies to holidays.

'People will customise the holiday to suit their needs and they won't pay for anything they don't use.

'Your holiday, your choice, is about the future of package.

'Since package holidays first came on the market more than 50 years ago the basic structure of the holiday – flight, transfer, accommodation – has stayed the same.

'We are bringing it up to date by offering a new level of service which means holidays can be tailored to suit the individual.

'The essence of the package holiday is that it's the best value for money, the most convenient way to organise a holiday and every package is backed by a raft of consumer protection, from health to financial bonding.'

Other features once considered part of a traditional package holiday, but are now charged-for extras, include late check-out and 'extra' baggage allowance.

Patricia Yates editor of the Consumers' Association *Holiday Which?* magazine said: 'People who are used to paying the price in the brochure for a package holiday will be in for a shock when they realise that things like coach transfers and airline meals are not included.

'This sort of tactic could backfire with the core group of people who book a package trip, because they expect everything to be taken care of.

'Clearly holiday firms are getting rattled by budget airlines who now fly to popular sunshine destinations.

'People assume a certain level of service on a package trip, and to charge for things like getting a hot meal on the plane may well be a mistake.'

© *The Daily Mail*
*April, 2002*

# Attitudes towards package holidays and ABTA

## Holiday destinations – 2000

Spain remains by far the most popular destination for package holiday makers in 2000. More than two in five package holidays from Great Britain were spent in Spain, some way ahead of the next most popular destination, Greece (16%). While Turkey has been rising steadily in popularity over recent years, the earthquake of 1999, coupled with reports of violence towards tourists during that year, have reduced its market share since 1998 from 9% to 6%.

Since the late 1980s, the pattern of holiday taking has not changed dramatically. Spain and the Canary islands have retained a remarkable consistency of popularity. Greece has grown in popularity over this time, as have other Mediterranean destinations (led by Turkey and Cyprus). This clearly shows that while world travel is becoming more widespread, and long haul packages are taking off, the Mediterranean remains the favourite spot for holidaying Britons.

While people may actually go to the Mediterranean on holiday these days, they dream of visiting Australia. It is the top choice destination, if money were no object, selected by 21% of all respondents. The United States (12%), Canada (4%), West Indies/Caribbean (3%), (plus other individual Caribbean islands, and occasional South American nominations) make the Americas the top dream holiday continent.

Fully two in five people say that they are 'certain' or at least 'very likely' to visit their dream destination, while just 5% think the opposite, which underlines the increasing accessibility of places which were once mere fantasies.

## Satisfaction

As in previous years, overall satisfaction with holidays remains high.

*By Andy Martin*

More than nine in ten holiday makers describe themselves as satisfied with their holiday (68% 'very satisfied'). Going back to 1988, this represents a significant increase in satisfaction levels. At that time, 51% of holiday makers described themselves as 'very satisfied' with their trip. Interestingly, however, the proportion of people who say that their holiday was unsatisfactory has remained virtually level at 5-6%, which perhaps indicates that some people are never going to be happy.

Value-for-money ratings have remained virtually constant since 1988. This year, 93% say that their most recent trip represented good value for money. More than half (56%) describe it as 'very good' value, although it should be noted that this falls to 43% of holiday makers aged 16-34.

### Booking a holiday

The proportion of people booking their holiday direct with a tour operator, rather than going through a travel agent, has again increased slightly this year, to 26%. This represents an increase of five percentage points since 1996, and has more than doubled since 1988, when the proportion was just 11%. With tour operators increasingly urging holiday makers to book direct, by placing their phone number prominently in brochures, it seems that this represents one of the major threats to travel agencies in years to come.

### The internet

This is the other major threat; much hyped, and now slowly beginning to take off. But how much will the internet affect the way Britons book their holidays? Although just 3% of holiday makers booked their most recent trip using the internet, 36% say that they would be prepared to do so within the next two years. At the moment, 56% have access to the internet either at home or work, predominantly through a computer. Two of the main reasons for not having booked the most recent holiday on-line are the desire for face-to-face advice (17%), and worries about security (14%), both of which are reassuring for travel agents. On the other hand, 15% say it was because they have only recently gone on-line, and 11% simply did not think about it at the time. As

## Travel agents

**How would you describe the overall service provided by your travel agent when you booked your last package holiday?**

| | 2000 | 1988 |
|---|---|---|
| Very good | 58% | 88% |
| Fairly good | 35% | 9% |
| Neither good nor poor | 4% | 2% |
| Fairly poor | 2% | * |
| Very poor | 1% | 0% |

Base: All who booked last holiday through travel agent (2000: 480, 1988: c750)

*Source: MORI*

internet travel advertising increases, and people become more confident about using the net (and spending money on-line), then it seems very likely that the internet will become a hugely popular booking methodology. Already 39% of all package holiday makers have used the internet as a source of travel information, and 17% have booked other forms of travel on-line.

### Travel agents

Most holiday makers feel that travel agents are becoming more trustworthy in their information provision. Three in ten say that their advice has become more reliable over the last five years or so, compared to just 5% who say it has got worse. As a consequence, almost nine in ten say that they are likely to reuse the same travel agent in the future. Despite this, however, the rating of overall satisfaction with travel agents has fallen somewhat over the last decade. The chart on page 9 shows that in 1988, fully 88% of holiday makers who had booked through a travel agent described the level of service as 'very good'. The proportion in 2000 has dropped to 58%. In that time, service level expectations have increased dramatically, and travel agents need to be aware that while very few people think their service is poor, the fact that so many now rate them only as 'fairly good' is an indication of possible trouble ahead.

One factor which might influence choices of booking methodology is the introduction of charges by travel agents, to compensate for the decreasing levels of commission they receive – particularly from airlines. Many are now contemplating making a charge to customers, for example, as a consultation fee. Although most holiday makers at present say that they would be likely to return to their current travel agent to book their next holiday, when faced with the prospect of paying up to £15 for a 30-minute consultation, just one in five say that they would definitely continue to book this way. More say they would book direct with an operator, or 'make their own travel arrangements'.

### Tour operators

As mentioned above, more holiday makers than ever are booking direct with a tour operator – up to 26% this year. The major reason for this appears to be the fact that so many operators are now printing direct booking numbers in their brochures. One in three people who booked this way say that this is where they got their information – a rise of 12 percentage points in only two years. Teletext also remains a very popular information source, cited by one in four, while the internet is starting to creep in, with one in eleven holiday makers who book direct using it for information on how to book their package holidays.

### Information sources

In recent years, there has been a shift in the focus of television programmes featuring travel. Few now concentrate entirely on the positive aspects of a destination, while some – such as *Holidays in Hell* – simply focus on the things that can go wrong. But what effect do they have on the travelling public ? It seems that they have quite an impact in influencing travel plans. Three in five say that as a result of seeing such a programme they might choose not to stay in a particular hotel or apartment, while almost half would avoid a resort if it came out badly in such a show. Only 13% of holiday makers say that nothing in any of these shows would affect their travel plans.

### ABTA

Over the years, ABTA has tested holiday makers' perceptions of what it actually does. As ever, in 2000, people are keen to use ABTA member tour operators and travel agents. They think this is an important safeguard, and many say that if the agency or operator they booked through this year withdrew its membership, they would not go back again in 2001. However, the proportion of holiday makers who strongly agree that it is important that their tour operator is an ABTA member has fallen from 54% in 1990 (when the question was first asked) to 39% this year, perhaps as a result of the lack of high-profile tour operator collapses in recent years.

Reinforcing this, there remains a great deal of uncertainty about what exactly it is that ABTA does. One in five holiday makers, for example, admits that they simply don't know (including 7% of those who believe it is important to book through an ABTA affiliated agent or operator). The most popular unprompted responses include the fact that ABTA offers protection to holiday makers, will help get you home if your operator goes bust while you are abroad, and operates an industry code of conduct. While 9% think that ABTA will also back holiday makers against the travel industry in disputes, 3% believe that the reverse is true. One in every fifty holiday makers, on the other hand, believes that ABTA is itself either a travel agent or tour operator.

### The environment

Environmentally conscious behaviour at home and on holiday appears to be fairly widespread (especially among ABC1s, and those aged 55+). Indeed, 85% of holidaymakers believe that it is important not to damage the local environment, while three-quarters say that their visits should include experience of local culture and food and 71% feel that tourism should benefit the people of the destination visited, through jobs and business opportunities.

Demonstrating their commitment to the environment, 84% of British holiday makers ensured that on their last package holiday they left no litter, and 63% visited a local site of natural beauty. Looking at practical and logistical measures, one in three saved water by showering instead of taking a bath, while one in five switched off air conditioning to save energy, and a similar proportion decided not to have their hotel towels washed so often for environmental reasons.

Perhaps indicating a growing awareness of the impact of tourism on the local environment, half say that they would be interested in finding out more about local issues (environmental and social) in their chosen resort before booking.

When asked how much extra they might be prepared to pay for environmental, social or charity guarantees, around half say that they would be willing to pay more to guarantee good wages for local workers, while two in five would pay more to ensure environmental preservation. A total of 81% of British holiday makers would be willing to make some sort of financial contribution for such guarantees. Among these people, the average amount that they would be willing to pay is just over 3%, which equates to around £15 on a holiday costing £500.

## Implications

After years of turbulent change within the holiday industry, it seems that as far as holiday makers themselves go, it's a case of 'plus ça change'. Popular destinations remain broadly in line with those which package holiday makers were visiting in 1988, and value-for-money ratings are virtually unchanged over the same period. People are, however, generally more satisfied with their holiday.

Holiday booking patterns are changing, although the much-heralded internet is yet to take a sizeable chunk out of the bookings market. The key shift at present is cutting out the middle man, by changing from booking in a travel agency to contacting the tour operator direct. Perhaps as people become more au fait with the travel industry, and with travelling in general, they feel that they have less need for specialist advice. Coupled with decreasing satisfaction levels concerning key elements of travel agents' service, therefore, this demonstrates a growing danger for those working in the traditional travel retail environment.

The travelling public remain very positive about the concept of booking with ABTA affiliated organisations, but also show very limited awareness of what ABTA actually does on their behalf. With so few recent high-profile tour operator collapses necessitating industry-led recovery plans, perhaps ABTA is beginning to fade a little from the limelight.

The environment is a key concern for many members of the public, whether at home or on holiday. The vast majority say that they would be prepared to pay a little extra for factors such as guaranteed levels of wages for local employees, and projects to minimise adverse impacts on the physical environment. Clearly, nobody is likely to spontaneously offer to pay extra for their holiday. However, this appears to indicate to tour operators that they would not necessarily lose out to their rivals if they were to instigate a surcharge designed to help protect the physical and social environments to which they send British holiday makers.

• This article describes the results of a survey conducted among package holiday makers by MORI, on behalf of the Association of British Travel Agents (ABTA). This is the ninth such survey since 1988 (of which all but the first have been conducted by MORI), during which time much has occurred within the industry itself; but how have holiday makers' attitudes changed? The article looks at how people taking package holidays in the new millennium regard their holidays, and map trends, to see how much opinions have altered since the late 1980s.

© MORI (Market & Opinion Research International Limited)

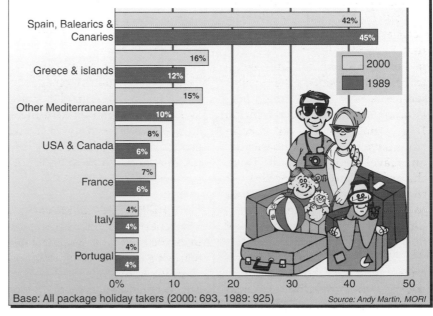

## Changes in popularity

**Spain remains by far the most popular destination for package holiday makers in 2000. More than two in five package holidays from Great Britain were spent in Spain, some way ahead of the next most popular destination, Greece (16%). Respondents were asked: 'Which country or countries have you visited on package holidays in the last 12 months?'**

- Spain, Balearics & Canaries: 42% (2000), 45% (1989)
- Greece & islands: 16% (2000), 12% (1989)
- Other Mediterranean: 15% (2000), 10% (1989)
- USA & Canada: 8% (2000), 6% (1989)
- France: 7% (2000), 6% (1989)
- Italy: 4% (2000), 4% (1989)
- Portugal: 4% (2000), 4% (1989)

Legend: 2000, 1989

Base: All package holiday takers (2000: 693, 1989: 925)

*Source: Andy Martin, MORI*

# Britons save by going abroad

*By Rosemary Behan*

A growing number of Britons is going on holiday overseas because it is cheaper than forking out to have fun at home, a recent survey by Teletext Holidays suggested this week.

A weekend in Tenerife can now cost up to £100 less than a weekend of 'pampering and partying' in Britain, according to the company, which says that four out of 10 holidaymakers book a holiday on the basis of price rather than destination.

Analysis by the company suggests that a typical weekend in London, for example, including a haircut, two nights out, food from the supermarket and one taxi ride, can cost as much as £248, while three nights in Tenerife, including flights, accommodation, food, drink and travel to and from the airport cost about £149.

Marc Bell, head of marketing at teletextholidays.co.uk, which carried out the survey, said: 'The increasingly great value of short breaks abroad means Britons are taking more holidays to destinations they have never been to before – and saving money in the process.'

Researchers analysed the amount spent on a typical weekend in Britain on food, travel and evening entertainment and compared it to typical offers for weekends in Majorca or the Canaries. Going abroad was a clear winner in terms of cost, even allowing for travel to and from the airport and entertainment at the destination. Over half (53 per cent) of the people questioned said bargain holidays were too good to resist.

> *'The increasingly great value of short breaks abroad means Britons are taking more holidays to destinations they have never been to before – and saving money in the process'*

This was borne out by the fact that 15 per cent of those aged 18 to 35 had been on at least three holidays in the past year – and a further 10 per cent of them had spent at least three weekends abroad.

Almost a fifth (18 per cent) of people aged 25 to 35 said they were 'addicted' to holiday deal-hunting. Mr Bell said: 'There's a new breed of UK travellers emerging and that's the dedicated jet pack.

'These people will spend hours trawling the internet for great deals, subscribe to travel newsletters and leave the country at the drop of a hat if the price is right – even if they know nothing of the destination. More often than not it's cheaper than staying at home.'

The survey showed that 17 per cent of holidaymakers expected to pay less for a trip away than a meal for two in a good restaurant.

Eight per cent admitted to spending two hours at work organising each trip, while 22 per cent visit a travel-related website once a week.

## International tourism

Growth in the normally buoyant tourism sector came to a standstill in 2001. International arrivals slipped by 1.3 per cent due to the weakening economies of major tourism generating markets and the terrorist attacks of September 11, according to the World Tourism Organization's preliminary results. International tourist arrivals totalled 689 million in 2001, compared to 697 million in 2000. But 2000 was an exceptional year for tourism, with special millennium events boosting international arrivals by 7 per cent and, in some cases, causing travellers to advance trips that would have been taken in 2001.

| Year | International tourist arrivals (millions) |
|------|------|
| 1998 | 628 |
| 1999 | 652 |
| 2000 | 698 |
| 2001* | 689 |

* WTO estimates

Source: World Tourism Organization (WTO)

# Responsible tourism

## Information from the Association of British Travel Agents (ABTA)

### What is it?

There are many definitions, but in a nutshell, it means making sure that tourism organisations look after destinations, so that their attractions and resources – whether natural or cultural – are not spoiled either for local people or for future visitors.

Responsible tourism means:

- Ensuring tourism cares for the environment
- Providing opportunities for local people to earn income e.g. from direct employment; by providing supplies to hotels; or by offering excursions
- Providing customers with appropriate information about the culture and environment of the destination to help them get more from their holiday.

### What the UK outbound travel industry is doing

Some companies, particularly independent tour operators, have practised responsible tourism for many years. Their tour programmes are designed to work closely with the people and the environment of the destination as an integral part of the holiday experience.

Responsible tour programmes include:

- Use of hotels that pursue good environmental practices such as conserving water and minimising waste
- Use of locally-owned hotels and transport companies that provide employment and income for the local population
- Hiring of local guides
- Providing customers with key information e.g. tips on dress codes, how to say a few words in the local language and important customs of the destination
- Supporting local community and conservation projects

For information about companies that incorporate responsible tourism into their programmes, visit:

- www.responsibletravel.com – ideas for more responsible holidays
- www.toinitiative.org – a United Nations responsible tourism programme, whose members include Thomson, First Choice, British Airways Holidays, Discovery Initiatives, Andante Travels, Exodus
- www.aito.co.uk – the Association of Independent Tour Operators (AITO) is strongly committed to responsible tourism and has many members who are leaders in this field. Find out about them here.

During recent months, key industry associations, including ABTA and AITO have been consulting with government, charities and campaigning groups working in tourism, to consider how the wider industry might incorporate responsible tourism into its business activities. It is likely that a new organisation will be established during 2002 to assist the industry to do this.

Future activities of the new organisation are likely to include:

#### For industry

- Tools to help companies pursue good practice e.g. encouraging hotels to conserve water and energy and obtain food etc. from local suppliers
- Training for staff internationally

#### In destinations

- Programmes to assist local businesses to work with the industry
- Support to local environmental and community programmes

#### For customers

- Providing information about things visitors can do to help the environment and economy in destinations and enrich their holiday experience

• The above information is from the Association of British Travel Agents' (ABTA) web site which can be found at www.abta.com

© Association of British Travel Agents (ABTA)

# The challenge of responsible tourism

## Information from the United Nations Environment Programme (UNEP)

Responsible tourism is the job of everyone involved. It is the job of governments and local authorities, the industry including training schools and hotel managers, of tour operators and the tourists themselves.

This was the message given by Ms Jacqueline Aloisi de Larderel, Assistant Executive Director of the United Nations Environment Programme (UNEP) at the World Travel Market 2001 WWF Environmental Debate in London today. The debate is the highlight of this year's WTM Environmental Awareness Day.

Ms de Larderel, who is also the Director of the UNEP Division of Technology, Industry and Economics, said the key question is how to put responsible tourism into practice. In this regard she highlighted how UNEP was responding to the challenge by providing practical tools for all parties.

'For governments and local authorities, we have developed policy guidelines and principles for the implementation of sustainable tourism. For tourists we have produced awareness-raising materials on sensitive ecosystems like coral reefs. With the tourism industry, we are both working with, for example, hotel managers and also the tour operators themselves. We must address the challenge at every level,' she said.

Highlighting a recently published teaching pack for the hospitality industry, Ms de Larderel said: 'Responsible tourism requires that decision-makers are made well aware of the impact of their activities on their environment, and of the solutions that exist. Providing tomorrow's hotel and tourism managers with environmental education is vital if we are to achieve progress.'

Ms de Larderel also said that the Tour Operator's Initiative has gone from strength to strength. Since it was launched last year, ten new members have joined the Initiative, taking the total to 25. The group now includes some of the biggest names in the industry such as: Accor Tours, British Airways Holidays, First Choice, Hotelplan, Japan Travel Bureau, LTU-Touristik Gmbh, Scandinavian Leisure Group, Thomson Travel Group and TUI Group. See http://www.uneptie.org/pc/tourism/industry/toinitiative.htm

Finally, with a reference to the current global economic downturn, Ms de Larderel said that at this difficult time for the tourism industry, it was more important than ever to protect the environment. 'We must not lose sight of the fact that a healthy environment is essential for tourism. We must all rise to the challenge of responsible tourism,' she said.

> *'Responsible tourism requires that decision-makers are made well aware of the impact of their activities on their environment, and of the solutions that exist'*

- The above information is from United Nations Environment Programme's web site which can be found at www.unep.org

© 2000, United Nations Environment Programme (UNEP)

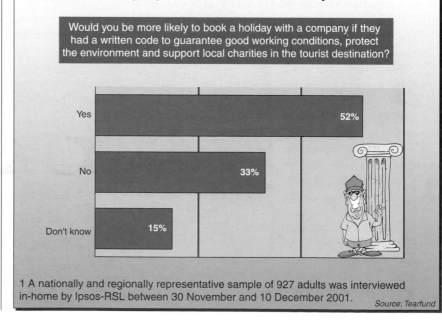

### Consumers want responsible tourism

**Attitudes are changing. New research[1] from Tearfund shows that the holidaying British public wants more information about how their breaks in the sun affect local people and their environment. They do not just want to switch off while on holiday. They are keen to behave in an appropriate manner and bring benefits to people in the destinations they visit.**

Would you be more likely to book a holiday with a company if they had a written code to guarantee good working conditions, protect the environment and support local charities in the tourist destination?

| | |
|---|---|
| Yes | 52% |
| No | 33% |
| Don't know | 15% |

1 A nationally and regionally representative sample of 927 adults was interviewed in-home by Ipsos-RSL between 30 November and 10 December 2001.

*Source: Tearfund*

# Ecotourism – hope and reality

## By Sue Wheat

*For those of us who are lucky enough to afford them, holidays are one of the most important things in our lives. And as the choice of travel increases people are increasingly looking beyond the traditional sun, sea and sand for other experiences. Ecotourism – tourism that takes you to fragile and beautiful areas – is one of the tourism industry's fastest-growing sectors.*

In 2000, international tourist arrivals reached an all-time high of 698 million, an increase of 7.4 per cent which was double the growth rate of 1999, according to the World Tourism Organisation. Receipts from international travel, excluding airfares, climbed to US$476 billion. Stated to be the world's largest industry, tourism employs 11 per cent of the global workforce – over 200 million people – either directly or indirectly. And as the population grows and incomes rise in many societies, the trend is expected to rise.

Even though the terrible events of September did lead to a fall in tourism numbers of around 11 per cent during the last quarter of 2001, the World Tourism Organisation (WTO) now forecast that the industry is bouncing back. They predict a long-term global annual growth of 4.5 per cent.

In 1993 the World Tourism Organisation (WTO) estimated nature tourism generated 7 per cent of all international travel expenditure. More recent research reveals this is now much higher, accounting for 20 per cent of international travel in the Asia-Pacific region and some areas, such as South Africa, experiencing a massive growth in visitors to game and nature reserves, of over 100 per cent annually.

## High spenders

Research by the International Ecotourism Society (TIES) reveals that ecotourists are likely to be higher spenders on their holidays than 'ordinary' mass tourists. And high spending, nature-loving, responsible tourists are undoubtedly an attractive option for governments looking for ways of earning foreign exchange.

But critics point out, just because something is marketed as ecotourism, doesn't necessarily mean that long-term protection of the environment is automatically supported through it. Even in countries which are well known as ecotourism destinations like Belize or Costa Rica the downsides have been obvious for several years. The fact that ecotourism businesses are often owned and controlled by outside interests, in just the same way as mass tourism, means that economic benefits often aren't used for the protection of the areas or to support the local community.

Osmany Salas, executive director of the Belize Audubon Society,

points out: 'Tourism proceeds are not being reallocated to the management or enhancement of the natural systems or to compensate local individuals who are adversely affected by the presence of protected areas.'

## Land speculation

One of ecotourism's first problems is one of definition. Although TIES has a definition of 'responsible travel to natural areas that conserves the environment and sustains the well-being of local people', there is no certification system to abide by or international monitoring body. The term can be used by anyone at any time for anything from a small-scale locally-run rainforest lodge where the money goes to support a local community, to a large, luxury, foreign-owned resort which has little community involvement and uses masses of natural resources. Ecotourists may even visit areas of national beauty and wildlife significance without realising that local people have been evicted from the area in order for ecotourism to be developed, as has happened in East Africa, India, Southern Africa and many other destinations.

With the growth in ecotourism, there are various changes ahead, says TIES executive-director, Megan Eplar-Wood. 'The original entrepreneurs will reach their market through the Internet with increasing efficiency. But the lack of discipline of government and the demand for growth will undermine efforts to create sustainable ecotourism economies that are small but beautiful. Overbuilding and land speculation will continue to destroy once tranquil zones.'

Ron Mader, who runs a Latin American ecotourism website, www.planeta.com, feels that eco-tourism should provide conserva-tion measures, include meaningful community participation and be profitable and self-sustaining. But he notes that such criteria are difficult to measure and quantify: 'Assuming you wanted to know which are the "best ecotourism destinations" the question must follow: how is one to judge?'

### Ecotourist 'year'

Many countries are now questioning how ecotourism is any better for local people than mass tourism. 'Two decades after it won independence from Britain, Belize finds itself yoked to another kind of colonial enterprise, the foreign-dominated ecotourism trade,' says Linda Baker in a report, 'Enterprise at the Expense of the Environment', for Environment News Network (www.enn.com).

Despite these problems, an International Year of Ecotourism (IYE) has been declared by the United Nations for 2002. This is being co-ordinated by the WTO and UNEP and a range of activities held, including the World Ecotourism Summit held in Quebec, Canada in May. Oliver Hillel, the UNEP tourism programme co-ordinator, sees the IYE as a chance to 'assess what ecotourism is, or can be, rather than only a promotional event for UN member governments, for the private sector and for recipients of development aid'.

The IYE has been met with enthusiasm by many tourist boards and tour operators. The Ecotourism Association of Australia, for instance, states that it 'recognises the un-precedented opportunity that this year provides, including benefits for nature tourism and ecotourism operators, the environment, indigenous communities, consumers and stake-holders involved with ecotourism'.

However, a coalition of NGOs, co-ordinated by the Malaysian-based Third World Network working with the Thailand-based Tourism Information Monitoring team (TIM-team), have stated vociferous opposition to the IYE. 'We are extremely concerned that this UN endorsement of ecotourism in light of all the fundamental problems related to the industry – in many cases another greenwash – will destroy more biodiversity and harm even more local communities,' says Chee Yoke Ling, of the Third World Network. 'That ecotourism is a viable strategy to replace other more unsustainable development activities is another myth that needs to be exploded.'

### Mekong plan

In correspondence signed by 29 international NGOs to UNEP, the coalition have cited various incidents where ecotourism is clearly working against local people and their environments. They cite examples throughout Asia, including the ecotourism policy promoted by the tourism working group under the Greater Mekong Sub-region (GMS) development scheme, led by the Asian Development Bank, which covers a vast area across Burma, Cambodia, Laos, Thailand, Vietnam and Yunnan/China.

---

*People talk about ecotourism, but the fact is that the tourism industry is always looking for a quick buck*

---

The GMS plan heavily relies on the construction of highways and entire cities dubbed as 'development corridors' as well as the building of airports, ports, large dams and other large-scale facilities. The ADB also revealed a plan to resettle 60 million ethnic highlanders from their homeland as part of a controversial watershed conservation project and to 'compensate' them with eco-tourism jobs in new locations. Given that hilltribe tourism has been fraught with problems relating to accusations of 'human zoos' being created and financial exploitation of hilltribe villages by outside tour operators, this option has been met with much derision.

The Third World Network also questions the long-term impact of promoting ecotourism. It is concerned about the lack of forethought over the impact of an ecotourism boom on environments and communities. And it questions how oversupply will be managed, the increasing link of ecotourism to the multi-million dollar biotechnology industry through biopiracy in key ecotourist sites like rainforests, and the use of ecotourism by the World Bank's Social Investment Project to support massive development projects, some involving logging operations.

In April last year, 100 angry villagers in Khao Sok national park Surat Thani province, Thailand, seized a bulldozer owned by the Royal Forestry Department and trunks of trees they had felled for construction of a 1000 square metre parking lot, an 800m-long road, 10 toilets and concrete stairs leading to a pier in the park. Campaigners point out that villagers get arrested if they collect mushrooms in the forest, or corals in marine parks, yet various World Bank-funded projects are allowed to fell trees and make landscape alterations without prosecution, despite it being against national law.

### Small operators

It is clear to many that nature-based tourism is presently seen as one of the most lucrative niche markets, and that powerful transnational corporations are likely to exploit the IYE to dictate their own definitions and rules of ecotourism on society. As a result, whole people-centred initiatives may be squeezed out and marginalised.

The commitment of the tourism industry to tackle these complex issues seems limited. Many smaller operators are keen to work closely with local people in order for the communities to support their business and out of an honest desire to protect environments and optimise benefits to local people. Many are working closely with community-run tourism operations, such as those listed in Tourism Concern's *Community Tourism Guide*. This describes various small-scale ecotourism successes. However, such operations make up a small proportion of overall tourism facilities.

'The mass tourism operators have learnt the language of sustainable tourism, or whatever you want to call it,' says Patricia Barnett, Director of the London-based

Tourism Concern. 'But little has really changed.' Proof of this, she says, was seen last year when the Balearic islands decided to implement an eco-tax of 62p per visitor per day to raise funds to correct the serious environmental damage done to the Balearics over the tourism boom of the last three decades and to protect fragile areas that are left. The international tourism industry threw up their hands in horror and lobbied fiercely against it, saying that it would damage business. 'We're not in favour of taxing tourists,' says Keith Betton of the Association of British Travel Agents. 'The Balearics should tax local hoteliers, who most benefit from tourism and are better placed to ensure that their elected representatives actually do spend the money in the intended way.'

This flies in the face of ABTA's own research, which revealed that 64 per cent of people indicated they were prepared to pay an extra £10 to £25 for their holiday if it went towards environmental or social improvements. 'It seems that when it comes down to it, the tourism industry just

doesn't believe that people will put their money where their mouth is, and, because they operate on such small profit margins, aren't willing to take the risk,' says Barnett.

An increasing number of commentators even within the industry are admitting there is something seriously wrong with the tourism industry and with eco-tourism. 'People talk about eco-tourism, but the fact is that the tourism industry is always looking for a quick buck,' says Doug Rhodes, owner of Hotel Paradiso del Oso in Cerocahui, Chihuahua in Mexico. 'Hotels throughout the Copper Canyon still lack waste treatment facilities. Some of the garbage is thrown into the canyon or disposed of near community wells.' But tourists are willing to pay for such environmental guarantees, he says, and waste management technologies aren't prohibitively expensive. 'It's just a matter of will.'

• Sue Wheat is editor of Tourism Concern's quarterly magazine, *In Focus*. A special edition on eco-

tourism can be previewed at www.tourismconcern.org.uk

Tourism Concern is a British membership organisation campaigning on ethical and fairly traded tourism. For more information, contact: info@tourismconcern.org.uk Or see their address details on page 41.

• The above article appeared in *People & the Planet* in May 2002. See their web site at www.peopleandplanet.net for further information. Alternatively, see page 41 for their address details.

# Air travel

---

## Information from Friends of the Earth

**W**e are flying more often to more destinations than ever before. Unfortunately, this increase in air travel is damaging to the environment and our health:
• Pollution and climate change
Aviation is one of the fastest-growing sources of climate change. Serious health risks also come from toxic nitrogen oxide emissions.

• Noise
The World Health Organisation has shown aircraft noise can cause stress and heart problems, psychiatric conditions and could impair children's ability to concentrate.

• Development pressures
Expanding airports add to road traffic congestion. Urban sprawl replaces our countryside bringing social problems.

### An industry that doesn't pays its way . . .
Air transport isn't subject to the same health and pollution regulations and taxes as many other forms of transport. For example, airlines pay no tax on fuel.

These favours distort the real demand to fly.

The end result is that every UK tax payer is subsidising the air travel industry – whether or not they fly.

### . . . and is out of control
*. . . we forecast for 2030 . . . 500 million passengers (a year) of which 300 million will be in the South East. These are very big numbers.*

John Spellar MP, Transport Minister, 9/4/2002

This is equivalent to six new airports the size of Heathrow. This would have a massive social and

environmental impact on the UK.

Where would they go? The decision is likely to be extremely politically controversial.

And it's completely avoidable. The Government should stop subsidising the industry and make it cheaper and easier to use less damaging forms of transport such as high speed rail.

Friends of the Earth says:
• Airlines and airports should pay for the problems they cause
• Huge air transport growth isn't inevitable – manage demand and explore the alternatives

• The above information is from Friends of the Earth's web site which can be found at www.foe.co.uk Alternatively, see page 41 for their address details.

# Worlds apart

## A call to responsible global tourism. A report from Tearfund

Tourism is one of the fastest-growing industries on the planet. In 1950 around 25 million people travelled abroad. In 2000 that figure was nearly 700 million.[1] The tourist industry employs 260 million people, and the World Tourism Organisation has predicted that by 2020, 1.6 billion people will be undertaking foreign travel each year.

- Globally, the tourism industry received £329 billion in 2000, an increase of 17% on 1995.

In the UK we are in the vanguard of this exploding horizon. Holidays abroad are no longer seen as luxuries. They are necessities. And as tour companies reveal ever more of the global holiday village in which we now live, we are looking to new exotic locations – including Thailand, Egypt, Brazil and South Africa.

- One in 10 holidays taken by British people in 2001 were to the developing world – a total of 4.3 million holidays.

But some of our favourite new destinations are also among the poorest countries on the globe. Places like India, Kenya, Nepal, Peru and Mexico, where millions struggle for survival on less than a pound a day.[2] These countries rely heavily on tourism and it can bring many benefits. But too often it brings negative effects or the benefits simply bypass poor people.

- In the Gambia, all-inclusive hotels cut out local traders. Yet UK holidaymakers spend an average of £834 per African holiday, over £120 more than the GDP per head in The Gambia.

New research by Tearfund reveals that holidaymakers do not want to enjoy themselves at the expense of those in destinations. They are willing to favour companies that can offer ethical guarantees.

- More than half (52%) of those questioned in a news survey by Tearfund said they would be more likely to book a holiday with a

company that had a written code to guarantee good working conditions, protect the environment and support local charities. This is a rise of 7% in the two years since Tearfund last asked the same question.

- Nearly two out of three people (65%) would like to know from travel agents and tour operators how to support the local economy, preserve the environment and behave responsibly when they go on holiday.

British tourists would like to know – and have a right to know – just how their holidays affect people in the destinations. And tour operators surely have a responsibility to tell them. Then holidaymakers can make informed choices about which company to travel with.

With a few notable exceptions,[3] tourism has been one of the slowest industries to adopt corporate social responsibility practices. Research in 2001 by Tearfund revealed that, of 65 tour companies, only half had responsible tourism policies – and many of these were so brief as to be virtually meaningless.[4]

- Many countries need tourism to survive. It has the potential to bring huge economic and social benefits to millions of people, including the poor. However, tour operators must now take their social responsibilities more seriously. They must also report more comprehensively on their practices in destinations, particularly in the developing world.

### References

1 *Tourism Market Trends*, World Tourism Organisation, 2001.
2 *Pro-Poor Tourism Strategies: Making Tourism Work for the Poor*, Ashley, Rowe, Goodwin, 2001.
3 Positive initiatives include the AITO Responsible Tourism Code, The Tour Operators' Initiative for Sustainable Tourism Development and the launch of responsibletravel.com.
4 *Putting Ethics Into Practice*, Tearfund, 2001.

- The above information is the executive summary of the report *Worlds Apart – A call to responsible global tourism* produced by Tearfund. See page 41 for their address details.

© *Tearfund*

# Top tourist destinations in the developing world (2000)

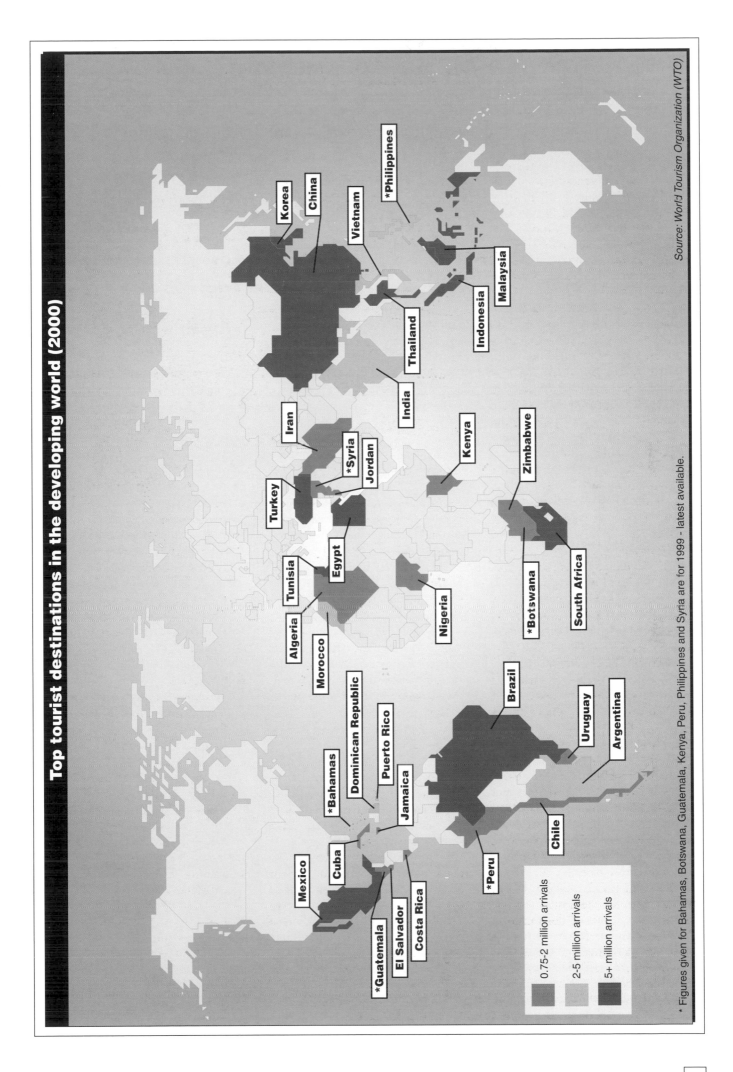

0.75-2 million arrivals

2-5 million arrivals

5+ million arrivals

Korea
China
Vietnam
*Philippines
Malaysia
Indonesia
Thailand
India
Iran
*Syria
Jordan
Kenya
Zimbabwe
Turkey
Egypt
Botswana
South Africa
Tunisia
Algeria
Morocco
Nigeria
Brazil
Dominican Republic
Puerto Rico
Jamaica
Uruguay
Argentina
*Bahamas
Chile
Mexico
Cuba
*Peru
*Guatemala
El Salvador
Costa Rica

*Source: World Tourism Organization (WTO)*

* Figures given for Bahamas, Botswana, Guatemala, Kenya, Peru, Philippines and Syria are for 1999 - latest available.

# Ecotourism

## Information from Tourism Concern

### What is ecotourism?

Ecotourism is a commonly used term internationally denoting 'nature tourism'. The term is used largely by the American public and tourism industry and less frequently by British tour operators.

The market for nature holidays has always been an important niche market in the tourism industry. Typical 'ecotourism' holidays include walking holidays, bird-watching holidays, mountain trekking, rain-forest trekking and safaris.

Ecotourism can be part of a more conventional holiday (day trips to areas of outstanding natural beauty) or can be a total holiday package where the tourist stays in a remote, rural environment for the duration of the holiday.

Ecotourism is a niche market: the World Tourism Organisation (WTO) estimates that ecotourism represents between 2-4% of all international travel expenditure (the same size as the so-called MICE segment – Meetings, Incentive, Congresses and Exhibitions).

Ecotourism is presently seen as one of the most lucrative niche markets in the tourism industry as ecotourists are higher spenders than 'ordinary' mass tourists. High-spending, nature-loving, responsible tourists are undoubtedly an attractive option for governments looking for ways of earning foreign exchange.

Ecotourism is often seen by poor communities as one of the few livelihoods they have open to them. Communities whose people are living in poverty invariably find their young people migrate to urban centres because of the decline in traditional industries such as agriculture and fishing. Tourism (often 'ecotourism' if they are in remote areas) can prevent this urban drift and provide an essential alternative income.

Ecotourism, if managed properly, could also be an important

**TourismConcern**
Campaigning for Ethical and Fairly Traded Tourism

means of protecting the world's rapidly disappearing ecosystems. If a natural area can be seen to have a higher financial worth as an eco-tourism destination than alternative more damaging developments, eco-logically important areas may be protected from deforestation, or agricultural or housing development.

Ecotourism is not, however, necessarily 'sustainable tourism' (see below). Sustainable tourism is defined as: 'tourism development that meets the needs of the present without compromising the ability of future generations to meet their own needs'. This means taking into account social and local economic factors, as well as environmental management issues.

'Tourism Concern is pleased that campaigning organisations in destination countries have pressurised the International Year of Ecotourism (IYE) to recognise that even ecotourism can have serious negative impacts on local people and environments and needs careful consideration,' says Patricia Barnett,

director of Tourism Concern. 'All tourism needs to benefit local people and their environments, including "ecotourism".'

### Tourism Concern's position on ecotourism

'While Tourism Concern is pleased that the impacts of tourism are being addressed by the international community through the IYE, we feel that ecotourism is such a small part of the tourism industry it will not make a significant difference to the sustainability of the overall industry,' Patricia Barnett says.

Tourism Concern has always pointed out that just because something is marketed as 'eco-tourism', doesn't necessarily mean that it supports long-term protection of the environment. This is true even in countries which are well known as ecotourism destinations like Belize or Costa Rica.

'Belize, for instance, is one of the world's best-known ecotourism capitals. However, it is something of a victim of its own success,' says Patricia Barnett. 'It now has a highly competitive tourism industry more interested in marketing a product than ensuring that it is environmentally sound, or that the people are benefiting

from it. Local people are marginalised as outsiders buy up the land. Locals are angry that they can no longer access their own forests, which have been their natural home for generations, and their islands are sold out to American ecotourism developers.'

## Greenwashing

Tourism Concern also notes that as ecotourism is undefined, it falls prey to 'greenwash' marketing:

'Ecotourism can be whatever anyone wants. There is no internationally accepted definition of ecotourism and there is no certification system to abide by, or international monitoring body.'

It also does not necessarily denote sustainability:

'The term can be used by anyone at any time for anything from a small-scale locally-run rainforest lodge where the money goes to support a local community, to a large, luxury, foreign-owned resort which has little community involvement and uses masses of natural resources,' says Patricia Barnett.

Tourism's vociferous appetite for basic resources – land, water and energy – has meant that the tourism industry and governments are increasingly finding themselves opposed over land rights and water rights by local people.

Ecotourists may even visit areas of national beauty and wildlife significance without realising that local people have been evicted from the area in order for ecotourism to be developed, as has happened in East Africa, India, Southern Africa and many other destinations.

## Problems with ecotourism: some examples

- Bolivia – environment: According to tour operators some self-described 'ecological hotels' around Lake Titicaca dump untreated wastewater into the lake. In the tropical Chapare region near Cochabamba, an immense area of jungle has been cleared to build a golf course for a five-star 'ecological hotel'. Bolivia, in fact, has no environmental standards for hotels (like many countries) and 'ecohotel' is a self-imposed title.

  (Source: Latin American Press)

- Botswana – people: The remaining few hundred Bushmen of the Central Kalahari are currently being forced off the land they have lived on for centuries by having their water supplies cut off. Intimidation and torture by wildlife officials has occurred. The Botswanan government has stated that (eco) tourists will not want to see 'primitive' people and the Bushmen lifestyle is not compatible with a developing country like Bostwana. Most of the Bushmen are now living in desolate camps outside the parks, reliant on food aid.

  (Source: Survival)

- China – wildlife: Research on tourism's impact in Wolong Nature Reserve in south-west China revealed that panda habitat was more rapidly destroyed than in areas not protected. Human population increased by 70% since the park was established to cater for the increased number of ecotourists. The number of pandas consequently dropped from 145 to 72 in 12 years.

  (Source: *Scientist* magazine)

- East Africa – people: Maasai and Samburu people in East Africa have been evicted from their lands in order for conservation and safari tourism to be developed.

  (Source: various, Tourism Concern)

- Thailand – environment, people: In April, 2000, 100 angry villagers in Khao Sok national park in Surat Thani province seized a bulldozer owned by the Royal Forestry Department and trunks of trees they had felled for construction of a 1000 sq. m parking lot, an 800m-long road, 10 toilets and concrete stairs leading to a pier in the park. Campaigners point out that villagers get arrested if they collect mushrooms in the forest, or corals in marine parks, yet various World Bank-funded projects are allowed to fell trees and make landscape alterations without prosecution, despite it being against national law.

  (Source: Tim-Team)

Tourism Concern also feels that the question of how to manage a rapid increase in demand for ecotourism must be addressed by the organisers of the IYE in order that environments and communities will benefit from the promotional year and not be overcome or marginalised by it.

Finally, the concept of environmentally-sensitive tourism cannot be fully addressed without dealing with the environmental impact of air travel. Air travel is one of the main causes of global warming.

'If tourists have to travel on several plane journeys in order to reach a remote ecotourism destination, can it be really be labelled as ecotourism?' says Patricia Barnett.

## Is the tourism industry taking environmental issues seriously?

Tourism Concern is very pleased that British tour operators and the British government have recently come together with British NGOs to develop a 'Sustainable Tourism Initiative'. This is a strategy for the entire tourism industry, not just those involved in ecotourism.

However, the commitment of the tourism industry to tackle these complex issues still seems to be limited.

'The mass tourism operators have learnt the language of sustainable tourism,' says Patricia Barnett. 'But little has really changed.'

Proof of this has been seen over the last two years in relation to the tourism industry's response to the Balearic islands' decision to implement an ecotax of 62p per visitor per day.

The ecotax has been decided on in order to raise funds to correct the serious environmental damage done to the Balearics by the tourism boom of the last three decades and to protect fragile areas that are left.

The international tourism industry, including ABTA, have lobbied fiercely against it, saying that it would damage business. This flies in the face of ABTA's own research, which revealed that 64% of people indicated they were prepared to pay an extra £10 to £25 for their holiday if it went towards environmental or social improvements.

'If the tourism industry are going to lobby against a small ecotax in a developed country, then we are not convinced that they are really committed to changing policies in support of the Year of Ecotourism. When it comes down to it, the tourism industry isn't willing to take the risk because it is so competitive and operates on such small profit margins,' says Barnett.

### A way forward

If ecotourism is to work, it needs to provide not only good conservation measures, but meaningful community participation too.

Tourism Concern has established an International Fair Trade in Tourism Network, which brings together tourism operators, NGOs working in tourism and communities in destination areas, to exchange views and information on socially and environmentally-sound tourism. By using the concept of 'fair trade', which has been so successful with other 'products' such as tea, coffee, bananas and crafts, we are attempting to find a way to make the tourism 'product' more fairly traded.

Tourism Concern has also published a unique guidebook for travellers listing community tourism projects, *The Community Tourism Guide*, many of which are ecotourism holidays. Importantly, all of these projects are either run or managed by communities and the profits from tourism used for community development, such as water, education and health facilities.

'The only way that ecotourism can be truly beneficial is for it to be community-based. Some tour operators do work closely with local people in order for the communities to support their business and out of an honest desire to protect environments and optimise benefits to local people, but they are definitely in the minority,' says Patricia Barnett.

'We hope that the International Year of Ecotourism will increase commitment amongst the tourism industry to be more community-focused in the their development of ecotourism.'

### Examples of community-based ecotourism:

- Namibia: one of the most well-known countries for community-based tourism and safaris where a wide diversity of ethnic groups has become involved in tourism usually by setting up campsites supported by private and public initiatives. NACOBTA (the Namibian Community Based Tourism Association) represents and promotes 21 community camps, museums and tour businesses. The profits from tourism are divided amongst the communities and tourism is managed by them for their benefit. www.nacobta.com.na
- Ecuador: Yachana Lodge was built by the Quichua community of Mondana. Visitors fish for piranha, swim in the Napo river and trek through the Amazon. Income from the lodge helps fund a health clinic, bee farm and permaculture farm. British tour operator, Tribes Travel, operates here working closely with the community. www.tribes.co.uk
- Kenya: Porini Ecotourism Ltd, a Kenyan-based tour operator working closely with Tropical Places in the UK, has developed a safari camp and relevant infrastructure with a Maasai community in Amboseli. Porini lease the land from the Maasai, pay the community a bed-night fee for every tourist visitor and train and employ local Maasai as game rangers, road maintenance staff, trackers and guides, camp attendants and drivers. www.porini.com
- The Gambia: normally known as a cheap winter-sun destination, The Gambia packs its charter tourists in along the coast, inland the country sees little benefits from tourism. The Tumani Tenda camp is a community-owned ecotourism project and its riverside accommodation is in low-impact, local-style houses. Visitors can get close to the local villagers who offer them boat trips, forest walks, crafts workshops, dance and music. Local small businesses, which have traditionally been marginalised by big international tourism players, have got together to provide local produce and services of a high standard to the tourism industry. www.subrosa.uk.com/asset/
- Thailand: hundreds of thousands of tourists visit the hilltribes in northern Thailand. It's rare for the guide to have permission to take tourists to tribal villages and little is done to ensure that the people visited benefit economically from the visitors or that their culture is respected. REST (Responsible Ecological and Social Tourism) trains hilltribe villagers on how best to manage tourism for their community. Villagers operate a home-stay programme for visitors and family houses receive tourists in rotation. Tourists are also given important cultural guidance about their visit. www.imaginative-traveller.com

• *The Community Tourism Guide*: Tourism Concern, Stapleton House, 277-281 Holloway Road, London N7 8HN. Tel. 020 7753 3330. Fax. 020 7753 3331. E-mail: Info@tourismconcern.org.uk Web site: www.tourismconcern. org.uk

• The above information is from Tourism Concern's web site: www.tourismconcern.org.uk

© *Tourism Concern*

# Ecotourism must become responsible tourism

**The upcoming World Ecotourism Summit - the culminating event of this, the UN International Year of Tourism - will hopefully go a long way towards ensuring that ecotourism is responsible and supports both wildlife and people . . .**

*By Justin Woolford*

Tourism is big business. As the world's largest industry, it currently accounts for more than ten per cent of global employment and eleven per cent of global GDP – and the annual number of tourist trips world-wide is predicted to double to 1.6 billion by 2020. The sheer number of people travelling around the world has a major, and ever-increasing, impact on both people and nature.

Mass tourism clearly is not sustainable. Inappropriate tourism developments and practices degrade habitats and landscapes, deplete natural resources, and generate waste and pollution. Ecotourism – defined by the International Tourism Society as responsible travel to natural areas that conserves the environment and sustains the well-being of local people – is often touted as the solution, as well as a panacea for sustainable development in communities that have few other resources.

But are current ecotourism developments always a responsible alternative? The building of roads, car parks, and accommodation in national parks is just one example of dubious ecotourism development. Lack of regulation has also led to ecotourism being used as a profitable marketing label for adventure holidays instead of an indication that tour operators are practising responsible tourism. In addition, some local communities have complained that they were never consulted about ecotourism development plans, or that the benefits fall short of what they were led to believe.

A deeper question is whether ecotourism is even desirable in some areas. A few ecotourists in a fragile environment may have a greater impact than hundreds of tourists in an existing resort – and may open the way for mass tourism to follow. In a similar vein, critics of ecotourism, such as the Third World Network, fear that if all holiday-makers become ecotourists, then hordes of travellers will invade villages and protected areas instead of staying in existing tourist centres – a development that could increase the undesirable impact of tourism rather than alleviate existing problems.

Recognising the impact of ecotourism – both good and bad – the United Nations declared 2002 the International Year of Ecotourism, offering all stakeholders the chance to review the effect of ecotourism on the environment and communities.

In the run-up to the culminating event, the World Ecotourism Summit, there have been a series of preparatory meetings around the world to discuss tourism in the context of conservation, communities, and marketing. The goals of the summit, which will be held in Quebec, Canada from May 19-22, include coming to a better understanding of the impact of ecotourism; improving its planning, management, marketing, and regulation; and ensuring equitable distribution of benefits to all stakeholders.

These are ambitious goals, especially since ecotourism involves a broad range of interest groups, from local communities and indigenous peoples to global corporations, national governments, and development agencies. However, given that

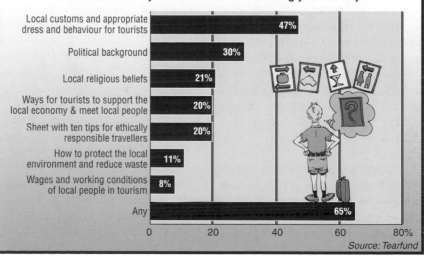

## When in Rome

**Nearly two out of three people (65%) would like to know how to support the local economy, preserve the environment, and information on local customs, politics and religious beliefs so they can behave responsibly when they go on holiday. This finding is up 2% on two years ago. It is backed up by independent research commissioned by ABTA in November 2000 which showed that 63% of those questioned would be interested in finding out about local issues before travelling and 70% think it is important that the holiday benefits the country you are travelling to.**

**If you were going on an overseas holiday, what type of information would you want to have concerning your holiday?**

| Category | % |
| --- | --- |
| Local customs and appropriate dress and behaviour for tourists | 47% |
| Political background | 30% |
| Local religious beliefs | 21% |
| Ways for tourists to support the local economy & meet local people | 20% |
| Sheet with ten tips for ethically responsible travellers | 20% |
| How to protect the local environment and reduce waste | 11% |
| Wages and working conditions of local people in tourism | 8% |
| Any | 65% |

*Source: Tearfund*

what's at stake is further degradation of the environment as well as damage to local communities, an ambitious plan is undoubtedly required.

Despite the critics, WWF, the conservation organisation, believes that responsible ecotourism does have the potential to support conservation and communities. But the organisation warns that ecotourism is no panacea. While it can provide an alternative to damaging economic activities such as logging and mining, there will be few instances where ecotourism alone can provide sufficient income to support conservation and people. The organisation believes that ecotourism should always be a part of a wider sustainable development strategy, and its growth carefully monitored.

WWF also warns that the existence of a wilderness area does not automatically mean that an ecotourism initiative will be successful. Success requires, amongst other things, good access, training, comfortable accommodation, visible wildlife, appropriate marketing, impact monitoring, and proper regulation. Many small-scale, community-based ecotourism initiatives have been set up only to fail due to lack of consideration of these factors.

The organisation believes that all tourism should maintain or enhance biological and cultural diversity, use resources in a sustainable way, and reduce over-consumption and waste, and is working on developing such responsible tourism practices at a number of different levels. One is to support community-based ecotourism enterprises where local communities have control over how ecotourism develops and gain an equitable share of benefits. Another is to push for certification programmes for tour operators. For example, the LINKS programme – initially a joint initiative of the WWF, the State of Alaska, and the Alaska Wilderness Recreation and Tourism Association and now an official project of the Arctic Council – aims to certify Arctic tourism businesses that operate in a socially and environmentally responsible way, and will assist in marketing these businesses to travellers.

A major, but often ignored, impact of all tourism is $CO_2$ emissions from air travel, which make a significant contribution to global warming and climate change. Realising that, in reality, few people will stop travelling in order to reduce their impact on the environment, WWF is promoting a new business tool that evaluates the environmental impact, or 'ecological footprint' of a holiday. The Holiday Footprinting tool estimates the environmental impact of a particular holiday by examining individual components – such as flights, waste, and food consumption – and then suggests 'scenarios' for impact reduction. In a similar vein, WWF is collaborating with the UK ecotour operator Discovery Initiatives, which pays a fee to a climate care scheme that invests in alternative

*The outlook here is promising – in a recent survey in the UK, for example, 85 per cent of respondents said they would like their holidays not to harm the environment*

technologies and renewable energy products designed to counter the impact of air travel.

Although certification, better regulation, and appropriate involvement of local communities will go a long way towards ensuring that ecotourism is responsible tourism, its future will ultimately depend upon travellers who support responsible tourism. The outlook here is promising – in a recent survey in the UK, for example, 85 per cent of respondents said they would like their holidays not to harm the environment. The growth of the ecotourism sector over the last two decades also appears to indicate a general interest in not damaging the environment while on holidays. The outcomes of the World Ecotourism Summit together with the work of organisations committed to responsible ecotourism will hopefully help raise awareness of the issues surrounding ecotourism as well as ensure that ecotourists are not inadvertently destroying the landscapes they come to visit.

• Justin Woolford was formerly Tourism Policy Officer at WWF-UK. He is now Toxics Campaign Leader at WWF-UK. The above information is an extract from WWF International's web site which can be found at www.panda.org

*© WWF International*

# Travelling with a clear conscience

**B**eing there, a travel magazine promoting 'ethical tourism', has been launched by the pressure group Tourism Concern.

'Eco-tourism': what a wonderful, conscience-salving word. It's a form of tourism that tour operators of all kinds have been offering us over the past decade so we can holiday in the knowledge that our rest and relaxation is simultaneously protecting the planet. If you're shooting photos of wildlife in the Masai Mara, it's a lot better than poachers shooting bullets. Or if you're gliding down the Amazon in a dugout canoe, you're being far less damaging than the hordes of tourists sitting in petrol-guzzling coaches.

There are now many examples of holidays that respect the environment. The fact that the eco-tourist tends to be a higher spender than the mass tourist also means that revenue can go into environmental protection. And increased understanding in tourists of the need to preserve the world's most beautiful places can only be a good thing.

But there is a growing sense, even within the industry, that 'eco-tourism' isn't all it's cracked up to be. Are we, in fact, being duped by the tourism industry's insistence that 'eco' must be 'good'? Some say we are. As one native Hawaiian on Kauai island told me: 'It's all very well hotels donating money to protect local wildlife, or having lights that switch off as the tourists walk out of their hotel room – but what's the point if the whole hotel is built on a sacred burial ground and depleting all our water reserves?'

In order for eco-tourism and conservation to be developed in East and Southern Africa, many indigenous people have lost access to their land and now live in poverty on the margins of the national parks. For reasons such as these, next year's UN-proclaimed International Year of Ecotourism has been met with some opposition.

### By Sue Wheat

We think it is time to look at the environment in its widest sense – people have to be put back in the picture. Wanting local people to benefit from our holidays made Tourism Concern look to the fair-trade and ethical consumer movements for guidance. If we can have fair-trade coffee and ethical pensions, can we also have fair-trade holidays and ethical tourism?

> ### Holidays that maximise benefits for everyone – guests and hosts – are undoubtedly the most enjoyable we can have

Protecting human rights and respecting local cultures is as important as protecting environmental resources. That means that tourism should provide decent jobs and pay reasonable wages; maximise local benefits; and not evict people

from their land to make way for safari tours, or divert water supplies to golf courses or hotels.

Tourism Concern's new magazine, *Being There*, seeks to show that ethical tourism is possible, easy, fulfilling – and necessary.

Some of the holidays featured are typically 'eco' – such as wildlife holidays in Kenya and Ecuador – but the difference is that all of them are owned or managed by local people so that they make money from tourism and can then feed and school their children.

What, then, is the willing tourist to do? There are some very simple questions that can be asked of tour operators and things to look for to sort the green from the greenwash.

Ask what sort of involvement in environmental and community issues your tour operator has, and check that it uses locally-owned accommodation and a hotel that is committed to sourcing its staff and supplies locally.

Make sure your guide understands that you are happy to abide by environmental regulations such as not going off-track on safari or not having a wood fire in areas like the Himalayas that are suffering from deforestation. And if you see something wrong with the way your operator treats local people or environments, speak up.

These are simple things. Unfortunately, the tourism industry still gets panicky when asked to clean up its act, saying that tourists don't care enough to want change. They have missed the point. Holidays that maximise benefits for everyone – guests and hosts – are undoubtedly the most enjoyable we can have.

• *Being There* is now available free with a £5 purchase from The Body Shop and Fairtrade shops around the UK. This article first appeared in *The Daily Telegraph*.

# Traveller's code

## Travel guidelines brought to you by Friends of Conservation

To enjoy your visit abroad whilst reducing the environmental and social pressures that tourism can bring, please observe the following guidelines.

### Before you go

With a better understanding of local cultures and traditions, your holiday will be all the more rewarding:

- Read a good guidebook or browse the Internet to find out more about your destination.
- Try to learn a few words of the local language, especially greetings. Local people will appreciate and respect your efforts.
- If you are thinking of taking tours, ask your tour operator for local information.

*When packing discard waste packaging – preferably for recycling – before you set off. This also means you can bring back more gifts and souvenirs!*

### Accommodation

Conserve local resources in your hotel, lodge or camp by:

- Turning down/off heating or air conditioning when not required.
- Switching off lights when leaving a room and turning the television off rather than leaving it on standby.
- Informing staff you are happy to re-use towels and bed linen rather than replacing them daily.
- Using water sparingly – a shower typically uses a third of the amount of a bath (although power showers use almost the same).
- Complying with any environmental initiatives your hotel operates.

*We use 70% more water on average than 30 years ago. Leaving a television on standby consumes up to 60% of the electricity used when watching it!*

### People and culture

Remember that you are on holiday on someone else's doorstep. Respect

the people and culture of the countries you visit, particularly less affluent countries:

- Avoid displays of conspicuous wealth, such as expensive jewellery. Aside from possible incitement to robbery, it accentuates the gap between rich and poor and may distance you from the cultures you have come to experience.
- Respect local people's right to decline to be photographed and remember that you may be expected to pay for the privilege to take their photograph.
- Wander though the local area and take an afternoon to meander away from the traditional tourist route. Consider hiring a local guide to take you round the sites as local people can often give insights into their area that you can't find in books.
- Ask your local agent about appropriate forms of behaviour, dress codes and how much to tip. Observe dress codes if you visit religious sites. Skimpy summerwear and public displays of affection may be inappropriate in some areas.
- Bargain if it is customary – but remember that the cheap price you pay may only be possible due to someone's low income. If you

do not wish to buy be polite but firm in declining.

- Take locally owned public transport (or if hiring a car, hire a small economical car). Buying local clothing, shopping in locally owned outlets and treating yourself to local food is a great way to get into the holiday spirit; also benefits the local community.

*Consider hiring a bicycle – this can be an excellent way of exploring an area and is an environmentally benign form of travel.*

### By the sea

- Beach rubbish is unsightly and can be dangerous to sea creatures. Some rubbish, such as plastic containers, takes many years to biodegrade. Please help prevent these fragile environments from being polluted further by taking your rubbish home with you.
- Leave pebbles, rocks and seaweed on the beach for others to enjoy. If you collect seashells please check it is not prohibited, ensure they are empty and take just a very few. If you do move rocks or seaweed carefully lift and replace them – there may be creatures underneath which need them for shelter.

## In the water

- When diving or swimming, avoid kicking up sand or stepping on coral, as it suffocates and kills coral polyps.
- Spearfishing is best left to those who need fish to eat, rather than as an exotic form of trophy hunting.
- Remember to watch out for wildlife and avoid wildfowl and fish breeding areas during breeding seasons. Respect wildlife reserves.
- Limit your speed if using jet skis and speedboats as riverbanks can be damaged from excessive wash.
- Avoid polluting waterways with waste food, litter, oil or any other material.

*Coral is extremely fragile and takes centuries to grow. Please don't remove any coral or cause any damage to this or any other living organism.*

## Safaris and nature trails

- Ask permission before entering indigenous people's territories, and pay properly for their services or handicrafts.
- Follow expert advice and heed safety warnings.
- Please keep to designated tracks, or ask your driver to, especially in National Parks and Reserves. Off-road driving can injure animals concealed in bushes or grass and interferes with their hunting. It also causes extensive damage to grass and woodland habitats.

*The animals you come to see are easily scared – so avoid bright colours and making noise. Encourage your driver to stop the vehicle engine when stationary.*

## Wherever you go

Please remember the following:
- Stay on approved footpaths when walking, marked routes when skiing, climbing or trekking and roads when driving.
- Don't contaminate local rivers, streams or springs by using pollutants such as detergents.
- Fire is a serious hazard. Be extremely careful with cigarettes and matches and take your cigarette stubs with you.

---

*With a better understanding of local cultures and traditions, your holiday will be all the more rewarding*

---

- Leave no litter. As well as being unattractive, it can take many years to biodegrade and have serious consequences on wildlife. Take your litter and dispose of it properly elsewhere.

*Protect wildlife and flora. Please don't pick flowers or pull up plants.*

## Ethical shopping list

Trade in many animals, plants and products made from them is controlled internationally to safeguard wild and endangered species.

- International trade prohibits the purchase of over 800 species and materials including: ivory, spotted cat furs, rhino horn, whales, sea turtles, many corals, reptiles, orchids and cacti. Check what your souvenirs are made from!
- Exotic souvenirs can threaten the most endangered species. Be careful if buying traditional Chinese medicines as these can contain products from tigers, rhinos and other protected species and are illegal to import.
- The purchase of exotic cat fur is ill advised as few are traded legally.
- Resist buying or collecting souvenirs from reefs such as coral, shells and starfish. In many areas this is prohibited, in some cases it is illegal or can only be bought with a licence. It contributes to the degradation of the reefs and marine life.
- When buying holiday souvenirs, remember that local crafts make unusual gifts and help to support the local economy.

## Facts for thought

- A 1997 survey of more than 240,000 plants indicated that 1 in 8 is potentially at risk of extinction. About 7000 species are at immediate risk.

- A species of animal or plant life disappears at the rate of one every 3 minutes.
- Every day an area of rain forest the size of Wales is destroyed.
- More than 50% of the world's coral reefs is at high or medium risk.
- Since 1970 a third of the natural world has been destroyed by human activity.

## Your holiday

While on holiday and after your return home, please pass on any concerns you have about environmental or social issues to your tour operator, local environment group or other organisation, as appropriate.

## Acknowledgements

The Travel and Tourism Conservation Group is gratefully acknowledged for its part in designing and distributing the FOC Traveller's Code.

This Group was established in 1991 by members of the travel industry and media to address the increasing concern that the travel industry and conservation were not working together to protect the resource base on which tourism relies.

The members are active in raising funds to preserve wildlife and ecosystems.

To access the members of the Travel and Tourism Conservation Group please check our website for an up-to-date list: www.foc-uk.com/PartnersNS.htm.

- The above information is from Friends of Conservation's web site which can be found at www.foc-uk.com

# Holidays

## Information from WWF-UK

Tourism is the biggest industry in the world, with massive impacts on people and nature. WWF is striving for responsible tourism – tourism that is beneficial to tourists and local people without harming the environment. You can help.

### Plan your holiday carefully

- Go on holiday during the off-peak period to prevent over-straining resources – you'll also avoid the crowds
- Find out about your destination before you go on holiday – it may be an environmentally sensitive area. Doing this will also ensure you are informed of what to see and any local customs
- Don't travel by air if you can avoid it – air travel uses up large amounts of fossil fuels and creates greenhouse gases
- If you travel by air, make a donation to Climate Care based on the length of your flight. This organisation supports the development of renewable and clean energy projects that reduce carbon dioxide emissions. Visit www.climatecare.org for more information
- Avoid taking things on holiday that you will throw away
- Dispose of any rubbish responsibly – it can be hazardous to wildlife

- Ask your travel agent or tour operator what they are doing to be environmentally responsible

### Be responsible in your accommodation . . .

- Turn off all lights, taps and air conditioning when you leave hotel rooms
- Re-use towels and participate in any green schemes run by hotels
- Dispose of sanitary waste properly. Don't flush cotton buds, condoms, tampons and plastics down the toilet – or you might just find them on the beach next time you visit

### . . . and when you are out and about

- Use public transport, cycle or walk instead of using a car
- Use facilities and trips run by local people whenever possible
- Don't participate in hunting or fishing unless it can be shown to be part of an effective management plan
- Don't be tempted to touch wildlife and disturb habitats whether on land, at the coast or under water
- When on holiday let the local people know that you appreciate pristine nature being there, so that they see its economic value
- Don't eat shark's fin soup or any

dishes you suspect of containing endangered species
- Be careful what you choose to bring home as a holiday souvenir. Many species from coral and conch shells to elephants and alligators are endangered because they are killed for curios or souvenirs. It is illegal to import over 800 species into the UK and over 25,000 more require a special licence
- Take all rubbish home from the beach – turtles are often killed by plastic bags they've mistaken for jellyfish and many items take years to degrade as well as being dangerous
- Boats and jet-skis create noise and chemical pollution which is disturbing to wildlife – don't keep the engine running unnecessarily
- If you are sailing, surfing or windsurfing keep a distance of at least 100m from seal resting and bird nesting sites to avoid disturbing them

### When you get home

- If you are concerned about anywhere you have been to on holiday, tell ABTA or contact WWF.

• The above information is from WWF's web site which can be found at www.wwf.org.uk

*© WWF-UK*

WOW! I JUST BOUGHT A CONCH SHELL!!

...I WAS HOPING TO SEE A LIVE ONE...

# Investigate your alternatives

## Information from The International Ecotourism Society (TIES)

**M**ore than 500 million people travel for leisure each year. Most travellers visit the same popular destinations – major international cities, national parks, monuments and ruins, and beach resorts.

Statistics tell us that mass tourism has a wide range of effects on the environment, culture and economies of local communities. Ecotravel offers an alternative to many of the negative effects of mass tourism by helping conserve fragile ecosystems, support endangered species and habitats, preserve indigenous cultures and develop sustainable local economies.

By looking at the alternatives and making informed travel choices, you can minimise your impact and positively contribute to the conservation of natural environments, local economies and cultures.

### Environmental impacts of tourism

Have you ever thought about what happens to a coastal environment when beachfront property is transformed into large resorts? What happens to prairies, forests, and the homes of wild and endangered animals? How does tourism affect the air you breathe, the water you drink, and the natural beauty that drew you to a destination in the first place?

According to recent statistics, the environmental impact of tourism development is of serious concern. In some popular destinations, the natural attractions of the area have been damaged or destroyed due to overbuilding and irresponsible development.

*Real-life problems*
- In popular resort areas like Cancun and Hawaii, overbuilt beachfront hotels have contributed to beach erosion, flooding and the disappearance of natural wetlands, generating mountains

of garbage without adequate means of disposal.
- Inadequate sewage treatment along coastlines of Brazil and many other countries causes the pollution of waterways, lagoons and the ocean, making local waters unsafe for swimming or fishing.
- In the Philippines and the Maldives, dynamiting and mining of coral for resort-building materials has damaged fragile coral reefs and depleted fisheries that sustain local people.
- In Kenya, safari activities have decreased wildlife populations, habitats and food supplies. Currently, the cheetah population is on the brink of extinction because nearby safari activities prevent the cats from hunting.
- In Nepal, the rapid growth of the trekking industry has increased pollution in Kathmandu and caused dangerous crowding and destruction of trails. Logging for hotel building materials and cooking fires has led to deforestation, flooding and landslides as far away as Bangladesh.
- In Yellowstone National Park, trash left by tourists has led to forced relocation of bears and their untimely death.

*What you can do!*
- Choose destinations that are not over-crowded or over-developed.
- Select responsible tour operators and guides who are aware of environmental impacts and contribute financially to conservation and preservation efforts.
- Seek out responsible, environmentally-sensitive accommodation.
- Follow all advisories, rules and regulations regarding protected areas, water sources and wildlife habitats.
- Take nothing with you and leave nothing but footprints.
- If viewing wildlife, never touch, chase or harass animals or marine life.

*Real-life models*
Tourism doesn't have to create negative environmental impact. In fact, many destinations and tour operators today realise the value of conservation and are altering their businesses practices to protect their natural resources and improve the environment.

In the Galapagos Islands, the number of ships allowed to cruise this remote archipelago is limited, and only designated islands can be visited, ensuring that visitors have little impact on the sensitive environment and animal habitats.

Cruiseliners in Antarctica now operate under strict self-imposed guidelines to limit the number of passengers and protect the seals, penguins and other wildlife from human impacts.

In Belize, a $3.75 departure tax goes directly to the Protected Area Conservation Trust, a Belizean fund dedicated to the conservation of the barrier reef and rainforest.

Ecotravellers can encourage these efforts by learning more about the environmental impact of tourism and making informed travel choices that support conservation and preservation of the natural wonders of the earth.

## Cultural impacts of tourism

As tourism expands and reaches the remote corners of the earth, its impact on local culture is inevitable. The influx of foreign values, money and goods alters the cultural landscape, sometimes permanently. Often that impact is negative, forcing locals away from their traditional lands, lifestyles and heritage.

### Real-life problems
- In Hawaii, culturally significant sites like burial grounds have been bulldozed and desecrated to make room for hotels and resorts.
- In East Africa, native Maasai tribespeople have been evicted from their traditional lands to make way for safari lodges and tours.
- In the Black Hills, the Sioux work as low-wage labourers in a white-owned tourism industry that promotes their culture and lands.

### Real-life models
Although tourism can have a negative impact, it doesn't have to be harmful to local people and their traditions. Around the world, ecotourism has helped conserve local control over land use, encourage local pride in cultural heritage and enable many traditions to be preserved or resurrected.
- The San of Namibia and southern Africa and the aboriginal peoples of Australia have recently regained management or ownership of traditional national park lands and conservancies, operating ecolodges and serving as guides and rangers while continuing their heritage.

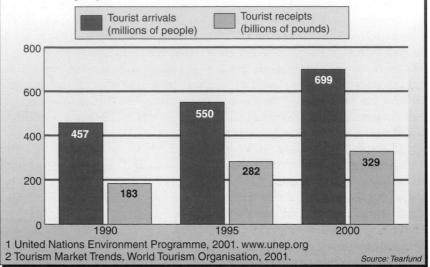

### Up, up and away – the growth of tourism

Tourism has come a long way since the advent of the jetplane and the creation of the comercial airline industry in the 1950s. Tourism is one of the largest industries and largest employers in the world. It currently accounts for 10.7% of the world's GDP,[1] and employs 260 million people. It is the number one ranked employer in Australia, the Bahamas, Brazil, Canada, France, Germany, Italy, Jamaica and Japan. It is the major source of income in Bermuda, Greece, Italy, Spain, Switzerland and most Caribbean countries.[2]

Legend: Tourist arrivals (millions of people); Tourist receipts (billions of pounds)

1990: 457, 183
1995: 550, 282
2000: 699, 329

1 United Nations Environment Programme, 2001. www.unep.org
2 Tourism Market Trends, World Tourism Organisation, 2001.
Source: Tearfund

- The Cofan peoples of the Amazon are running an ecotourism enterprise in their territory where they sustain a thriving home-based craft industry for local visitors, while conserving and sharing their language, shamanic culture, and traditional knowledge of medicinal plants.

### Whay you can do!
- Choose destinations that are not over-crowded or over-developed.
- Seek out tour operators and accommodation that are sensitive to the local culture.
- Educate yourself about your host country's customs before travelling. Remember that you are a guest and behave accordingly.
- Check local conventions and dress appropriately.
- Be sensitive to where, how and when you take photographs. Always ask first.
- Be respectful of local people's

---

*Seek out tour operators and accommodations that are sensitive to the local culture*

---

peace, privacy and land. Ask permission before entering buildings, shrines or sacred lands.
- Learn a few words of the local language and use them when meeting people. Speaking to locals in their language will demonstrate your respect for local culture.
- Attend local cultural events. Your support helps local performers preserve their heritage.
- When purchasing souvenirs, support the work of local craftspersons and artisans. Help keep cultural traditions alive.

Ecotravellers can support the preservation of local culture by educating themselves about the cultural impact of tourism and making informed travel choices that minimise their impact on the people they visit.

## Economic impacts of tourism
Tourism is the world's largest and fastest-growing industry. According to recent statistics, tourism provides 10 per cent of the world's income and employs almost one-tenth of the world's workforce. By the year 2010, these numbers will double. All considered, tourism's actual and potential economic impact is astounding. But there are also negative sides of tourism's economic boom.

*Real-life problems*

- In most all-inclusive package tours, more than 80 per cent of travellers' fees go to the airlines, hotels and other international companies, not to local businesses or workers.
- Large hotel chain restaurants often import food products to satisfy foreign visitors and rarely employ local staff for senior management positions, preventing local farmers and workers from reaping the benefit of their presence.
- Resorts and hotels often over-consume natural resources like water and power, forcing utility prices up and causing blackouts and water shortages for locals.
- Hotel shops often import or buy mass-produced gift items instead of those produced by local craftspeople and artisans.
- Many tourists never leave the hotel grounds or cruise ship, reducing the possibility of tourist income for local businesses.
- Faced with limited economic prospects, locals lose the incentive to preserve and conserve their natural and cultural resources.

### What you can do!

- Choose locally-owned and operated lodges, hotels, tour guides. Take advantage of local taxis, buses and car rental agencies.
- Support local and international tour companies and accommodation that employ local people and purchase locally-grown foodstuffs.
- Eat in local restaurants and shop in local markets.
- Purchase souvenirs from local shops and artisans.
- When paying locals for goods or services, make every effort to offer a fair price.
- Pay access fees to protected sites, even when voluntary. Your money supports local efforts to conserve those areas.
- Frequent local cultural events. Your money helps local artists and performers and encourages preservation of cultural heritage.

*Real-life models*

Fortunately, the negative economic effects of tourism can be mitigated. Through sensitive development practice and the financial support of tourists, locals in St Lucia, Vietnam, Tanzania and Peru, among other places, are participating in a sustainable tourist economy via locally-owned hotels, tour companies, wildlife park management and farming cooperatives that supply food to hotels and resorts.

- Women in the booming trekking regions of Nepal are emerging from tea house kitchens to become guides and lodge owners with the help of a community tourism programme that provides funds and training.
- In Natal, South Africa, the park service works to ensure that villagers have free access to parks for local needs and have the opportunity to sell their handicrafts at local lodges. Proceeds from the sale of handicrafts make it possible for parents to buy better clothing and school supplies for their children.

Ecotravellers can support vital efforts like those above by making informed travel choices. Spending wisely can help create better opportunities for local businesses, farmers and artisans, while fostering sustainable economic growth and providing genuine benefit to the people in vacation destinations.

- The above information is from The International Ecotourism Society's (TIES) web site which can be found at www.ecotourism.org

© The International Ecotourism Society (TIES)

# Green tax helps islands clean up

### By Giles Tremlett

British holidaymakers checking into resorts in Spain's Balearic islands will today become among the first people in the world to pay a controversial green tourism tax, designed to reverse damage done by 30 years of tourism.

Visitors to Majorca, Ibiza, Menorca and Formentera will have to pay an average of one euro a day each towards the tax when they check out of hotels, hostels or campsites.

Regional authorities say the tax will fund a £40m-a-year environmental fund to protect the natural beauty of the archipelago. Critics respond that wealthy islanders are simply making today's visitors pay for their past greed, when they tried to squeeze as many tourists as possible on to their beaches each summer.

Authorities said the ring-fenced tax would be spent on projects such as buying and demolishing ugly hotels in towns such as Calvia, in northern Majorca, and turning the land they are on into parks.

The local government's environment department says the money is needed to cope with the damage caused by 12 million visitors a year, mainly from Britain and Germany.

Although the spending will be overseen by a committee that includes environmental groups, the law would also allow spending on tourism infrastructure – a fact which has been criticised by some.

The islands' government insists the money will not fund roads or airports, but it has talked of building museums.

The new tax has also angered the tourist industry and some visitors. Hotel owners blame it for a 5% fall in bookings from Germany this year. UK bookings have also fallen, although this is partly because more people are buying second homes on the islands.

© Guardian Newspapers Limited 2002

# Over paid, over sexed, over there

*By Oliver Bennett*

*If tourism were a country it would have the second largest economy in the world after the US. As more of us travel further afield in pursuit of pleasure, Oliver Bennett describes how the way we conduct ourselves – and the type of holiday we choose – can make all the difference to our hosts.*

Do you feel rich? My guess is that there are not many of you who would say they do. Yet the chances are that your income is greatly more than £235 a year. Ten times as much? Or a hundred times as much? There must be a few people who would admit to earning £23,5000. Or could it be even more? Two hundred times as much? Still less than £50,000 a year.

But £235 a year is an income of about one US dollar day. This is a yardstick for absolute poverty used by the international community. And the figure they are talking about is a maximum income; for most people it will be less.

What has this got to do with tourism? Some would say 'not much'. There is a view that you, the rich visitor to a foreign destination, cause social disruption even by merely displaying your wealth. The camera you thought was cheap is expensive to someone with an income of less than a dollar a day – and you will take your camera won't you? And perhaps by now you can see that maybe you are richer than you thought.

Social damage, environmental destruction. Destroying the coral

reefs. Upsetting a way of life by even unwittingly imposing yours. In the Mustang area of Nepal, only opened to tourism in the 1990s, one comment made of visitor behaviour always sticks in my mind;

'In your home country, people don't stick their cameras through the window of a house, do they? So why do they do it into mine?' Sobering question indeed.

But there is another side to tourism. For quite a few countries around the world there are not that many economic options. Agriculture and fishing may be among them. Yet there may be growing urban populations, young people who cannot find jobs or even if they can earn an extremely modest income. More traditional forms of securing an income may not be an option.

Once, in Botswana, I visited the home of my security guard. It turned out to be a cardboard box, labelled 'Gift of the people of the United States of America'. I am sure he would have preferred a better job, a higher income.

Many development agencies view tourism as a frivolous activity. Something that doesn't merit their support. And if all the donor aid achieves is a subsidy for the rich visitor (maybe you) then of course they would be right.

Earlier this year I was one of a team tasked by the UK Department for International Development to look at the issue of tourism and poverty elimination. One of the targets set in the 1997 UK White Paper on international development is to halve the proportion of people living in extreme poverty (an income of less than one US dollar a day) by 2015. Is tourism frivolous or is there a role for it to play is achieving this objective?

I believe the answer is 'yes'. It is not a black and white answer. It depends where it is, that the alternative development options are, how it is done.

Eighty per cent of the world's poor people live in one of twelve countries. In eleven of these, tourism is significant and/or growing. The issue then is how to connect tourism (which may be international or domestic) with the poor. How can they derive benefits from it? One way is to use money from tourism to assist in projects.

For example, money from the charge made to enter Mustang in Nepal has gone to such things as mini hydro-electric schemes so that people have electricity where there was none before. The German tour operator, Studiosus Reisen, puts money earned from their clients into a string of development projects around the world. The Austrian operator Imholz Reisen have a 'Tourism for Development' programme whereby $1 per person per night in Egypt goes to a specially established fund, which is independently audited and is spent on village development.

But this kind of help is something of paternalism. It requires someone deciding how to spend the money. It is not empowering people by giving them income they have earned directly into their pockets.

A common reaction to this is to think of community based tourism. It may be tour guiding linked to maintaining a cultural heritage attraction. It may be a simple rest camp. But these are often not simple solutions.

Tow work they need to be linked into the conventional tourist industry. Well-meaning support organisations can get things wrong because they have insufficient understanding of how the tourism industry functions. So visitors may simply not know an attraction is there. Tour operators may pass it by.

A while ago we, as European tax payers, funded the restoration of a fort in Fiji. To my mind it is the best heritage attraction on the main island. To have a Fijian show you where one of your forebears was prepared prior to being eaten is an unusual experience to say the least. Yet not many tours go there. When the opening ceremony was due the village up the valley decided that the site was on their land. The nearer village was sure it was theirs. Because of this dispute the opening was cancelled ('though we still had the feast', I was told, 'as everything was ready'). And as with other schemes elsewhere, follow-on training was lacking. Training on how to market the attraction for instance.

For community based tourism projects to be effective can require a lot of outside help. Maybe not money but time, or technical assistance as it is known. But then such projects do not necessarily help the poorest. To set them up requires some form of capital. To operate them successfully requires some appreciation of the basics of running a business enterprise. And what can be an enormous gulf between your expectations as a visitor and their appreciation of those expectations has to be bridged.

So what can help the poor? There are opportunities for very small businesses which may be informal enterprises, supplying goods or produce to tourism businesses or producing handicrafts. And they need to be given a chance. Local tour companies can tour guides may ignore them, the tour bus flashes by simply because a more sophisticated (and expensive) outlet pays commission to the tour guides.

Equally important is that the poor are involved. Avoiding destruction to their local environment. Ensuring that tourism does not trample on their livelihoods, swamp their fishing grounds for instance. When there is communication between communities and tourism interests it is much better than when there is not. And the foreign tour industry, from airlines and tour operators to guide book authors, can engender an appreciation of local culture among their customers and readers.

You may well say 'what has this got to do with me?'

Should you be involved in tour operation, you can reflect on the worlds of Dr Wolf Iwand, Director of Environment at leading German tour operators TUI. He said at this year's ITB in Berlin:

'The global industries and global companies must shoulder responsibility. Responsibility for an equitable balance between north and south, west and east. Responsibility for providing equal opportunities and fighting poverty because the consequences of inequality and poverty are among the greatest threats to the social environment. Because the social limits to growth are reached much sooner than the environmental limits.'

---

### *Eighty per cent of the world's poor people live in one of twelve countries*

---

While some British tour operators have taken environmental conservation on board as an objective, very few have gone one step further and done anything about addressing the social development issues that TUI has identified.

If you are not in tour operating, you may be in education. Issues of the role tourism can play towards poverty elimination can be included in your curricula. If you are not in education, perhaps you are in government or a business which focuses solely on the UK market. You may not be able to spend time working abroad for Voluntary Service Overseas (VSO) or British Executive Service Overseas, but maybe you could do something. Could you work in a group rather than as an individual in providing voluntary hands-on support to a project overseas? Or if you are in business think about whether you could form a partnership with an enterprise in a developing country. You may not know that there is a Business Partnership Unit in the Department for International Development which can play a support role in such ventures.

• Oliver Bennett is a consultant for Deloitte & Touche. You can find information on responsible breaks in *The Community Tourism Guide*, published by Earthscan for Tourism Concern, www.earthscan.co.uk Additionally, DFID publish *Changing the Nature of Tourism*, available from the Public Enquiry Point on 0845 3004100.

• The above article originally appeared in *Developments* magazine (www.developments.org.uk), produced by the Department for International Development (DFID). See page 41 for their address details.

*© Department for International Development (DFID)*

# Pro-poor tourism

## Harnessing the world's largest industry for the world's poor

Tourism is one of the world's largest industries, generating an estimated 11%[1] of global Gross Domestic Product (GDP), employing 200 million people and transporting nearly 700 million international travellers per year – a figure that is expected to double by 2020. Developing countries currently have only a minority share of the international tourism market (approximately 30%) but this is growing. International tourism arrivals in developing countries have grown by an average of 9.5% per year since 1990, compared to 4.6% worldwide. The tourism industry makes important contributions to the economies of developing countries, particularly to foreign exchange earnings, employment, and GDP.

Tourism is clearly of great significance to developing countries. But is it important in those countries with the highest proportion of poor people? The small island economies which are most dependent on tourism tend to be middle income and contain few of the world's poor. Nevertheless, analysis of tourism data shows that in most countries with high levels of poverty, tourism is significant or growing. Tourism is therefore a fact of life for many of the world's poor.

A reduction in world poverty is an internationally agreed priority and targets have been set to halve poverty by the year 2015. Achieving poverty reduction requires actions on a variety of complementary fronts and scales, but a prerequisite of significant progress is pro-poor growth – growth which benefits the poor. As an industry that is clearly important in many poor countries, can tourism be one source of such growth?

### Can tourism benefit the poor?

Sceptics argue that because tourism is often driven by foreign, private sector interests, it has limited potential to contribute much to poverty elimination in developing

*By Dilys Roe, UK, and Penny Urquhart, South Africa*

countries. It is noted for high levels of revenue 'leakage', and of the revenue that is retained in the destination country, much is captured by rich or middle-income groups – not the poor. Tourism is also a volatile industry, being extremely susceptible to events which are difficult to control – political unrest, exchange rate fluctuations, natural disasters. The recent foot and mouth outbreak in the UK is an obvious example of the speed and severity with which a national tourism industry can be affected by events outside its control. In poor countries, tourism can have a particular effect on the poor themselves, causing displacement, increased local costs, loss of access to resources and social and cultural disruption.

> *Tourism is clearly of great significance to developing countries. But is it important in those countries with the highest proportion of poor people?*

However, many of the supposed disadvantages of tourism are in fact common to many types of economic development in a globalising world while many of the advantages do appear to have greater pro-poor potential:

- It is a diverse industry. This increases the scope for wide participation, including the participation of the informal sector
- The customer comes to the product, providing considerable opportunities for linkages (e.g. souvenir selling)
- Tourism is highly dependent upon natural capital (e.g. wildlife, scenery) and culture. These are assets that some of the poor have, even if they have no financial resources
- Tourism can be more labour intensive than manufacturing (though less labour intensive than agriculture)
- Compared to other modern sectors, a higher proportion of tourism benefits (jobs, petty trade opportunities) go to women

Given that tourism is already a fact of life for many of the world's poor, whether or not it is more or less pro-poor than other sectors is perhaps irrelevant. The challenge is to enhance the many positive impacts it can have and reduce the costs it can place on the poor.

### Pro-poor tourism and sustainability

The World Tourism Organisation defined sustainable tourism as early as 1988 as 'leading to the management of all resources in such a way that economic, social and aesthetic needs can be fulfilled while maintaining cultural integrity, essential ecological processes, biological diversity and life support systems'. However, to date, much of this debate has focused around environmental sustainability or enhancing community involvement in tourism. While many initiatives incorporate pro-poor elements, this approach to 'sustainable tourism' fails to take into account the links between poverty, environment and development. In a world of growing inequality, there can be no doubt that attacking poverty is a critical component of sustainable development. Significantly though, the 1999 meeting of the UN Commission on Sustainable Development urged governments to: 'Maximise the potential of tourism for eradicating poverty by developing appropriate strategies in co-operation with all major groups, indigenous and local communities.' Pro-poor tourism attempts to do this, putting poor people and poverty at the centre of the sustainability debate.

Pro-poor tourism (PPT) is defined as *tourism that generates net benefits for the poor*. Benefits may be economic, but they may also be social, environmental or cultural. Pro-poor tourism is not a specific product or sector of tourism, but an approach to the industry. Strategies for making tourism pro-poor focus specifically on *unlocking opportunities* for the poor within tourism, rather than expanding the overall size of the sector. Three core activities are needed: increasing access of the poor to economic benefits (by expanding business and employment opportunities for the poor, providing training so they are in a position to take up these opportunities and spreading income beyond individual earners to the wider community); addressing the negative social and environmental impacts often associated with tourism (such as lost access to land, coastal areas and other resources and social disruption or exploitation); and policy/process reform (by creating a policy and planning framework that removes some of the barriers to the poor, by promoting participation of the poor in planning and decision-making processes surrounding tourism, and by encouraging partnerships between the private sector and poor people in developing new tourism products.

## How can pro-poor tourism be supported?

Government, the private sector, non-governmental organisations, community organisations and the poor themselves all have critical and very different roles to play in pro-poor partnerships. At a minimum, private operators should participate in product and market development to ensure commercial realism. There is much that only governments can do, so a leading role for government in PPT is a great advantage. At a minimum, there needs to be a policy environment that facilitates PPT. The poor themselves are critical to PPT, but they often also need to be organised at the community level in order to engage effectively in tourism. It is often invaluable to have a fourth party to catalyse and support PPT efforts of others – this is often, though not always, a role for a non-governmental organisation. Donors, through their role in supporting tourism plans, and the 'sustainable tourism' agenda, can also promote PPT.

---

*Pro-poor tourism is defined as tourism that generates net benefits for the poor. Benefits may be economic, but they may also be social, environmental or cultural*

---

Early experience shows that PPT strategies do appear able to 'tilt' the industry, at the margin, to expand opportunities for the poor and have potentially wide application across the industry. Poverty reduction through PPT can therefore be significant at a local or district level. National impacts would require a shift across the sector, and will vary with location and the relative size of tourism. This would be a challenge indeed, but surely a challenge worth rising to?

### Reference

1  This figure is commonly quoted by the World Travel and Tourism Council (WTTC) although the World Tourism Organisation (WTO) puts the figure much lower. The difference reflects the difficulty in defining what is and is not included within the tourism 'industry' and whether services such as transport are included in the calculation. The WTTC figure also incorporates the multiplier effect of tourism spending and so reflects the wider 'tourism economy' rather than just the industry itself.

• The above information is an extract from *Pro-poor tourism – Harnessing the world's largest industry for the world's poor* produced by the International Institute for Environment and Development. See page 41 for their address details.

*© International Institute for Environment and Development (IIED)*

# Holidays abroad needn't cost the Earth

## Information from WWF-UK

A new report commissioned by WWF reveals that a typical Mediterranean holiday can account for up to 50 per cent of a person's annual share of the Earth's natural resources.

Using a new practical business tool developed for WWF, consultants were able to evaluate the environmental impact or 'ecological footprint' of two summer holiday packages to Majorca and Cyprus, based on data provided by Thomson Holidays. The system uses the concept of 'area units' to quantify the Earth's natural resources. Each person on the planet can use up to two of these area units per year without damaging the environment.

According to the calculations, the Majorca holiday used 0.03 area units per night, while the Cyprus holiday accounted for 0.07. Over the course of the two weeks, this added up to a total of 0.37 units and 0.93 area units respectively – 20 per cent and 50 per cent of an individual's 'fair share' of resources for one year. As a financial analogy, this is the equivalent to spending 20 or 50 per cent of your entire annual income in just one two-week period.

### Opportunities for savings

However, the new tool doesn't just highlight the potential impact of a holiday abroad, it also shows that, by taking a few simple measures to make holidays more environmentally friendly, tour operators, holiday-makers and hoteliers can actually save money. It allows a tour operator to estimate the environmental impact of a particular holiday by examining individual components such as flights, waste and food consumption, and then suggests 'scenarios' for impact reduction.

WWF's tourism officer, Justin Woolford, said: 'There is increasing pressure on the tourism industry to be more transparent and responsible. Because it takes an overview of the whole holiday product, this tool is a great way of communicating and improving environmental performance.'

Although holidays can be an extremely expensive proposition in environmental terms, short-haul trips, to the Mediterranean at least, fit within an individual's annual fair share of resources. But this requires that we lead a low-impact existence outside the holiday period. Currently this is not the case. In the UK, each person uses around 6.8 units each year – more than three times their fair share.

### Air travel

Flights are the largest contributor to the environmental impact of a holiday, accounting for 56 per cent of the Majorca trip and 46 per cent of the Cyprus trip. Waste was responsible for a quarter of the Majorca holiday footprint, and for 35 per cent for Cyprus. Food consumption accounted for nine per cent of the Majorca footprint, while excursions made up six per cent in Cyprus.

Although few people will stop taking holidays abroad in order to reduce their environmental impact, a few simple steps can mean that the same holiday is more environmentally friendly and can lead to savings for all parties.

Improved air traffic control and aircraft occupancy rates can reduce the impact from burning aviation fuel. In hotels, solar power and provision of more dairy food, fruit, vegetables, seafood and fish products and less meat, can also reduce impacts. Locally produced goods also reduce the demand for air fuel, as fewer items need to be brought in from abroad.

Craig Simmons, Director of Best Foot Forward, the consultancy that carried out the study, said: 'Footprinting shows that business and the environment can both be winners – it helps a company to see where its impacts lie and suggests ways to reduce consumption, saving both planet and pocket.'

### Sustainable development

WWF calls on all tour operators to adopt the holiday footprinting tool in the pursuit of more responsible tourism. Tourism that is more sensitive to the environment can make a significant contribution towards the goal of sustainable development – how we provide resources to meet demand today without reducing the resources available for tomorrow.

Sustainable development is the crucial issue at the forthcoming World Summit on Sustainable Development in Johannesburg, the successor to the 1992 Rio conference. One key element to help achieve this is to cut back on pollution and wasteful consumption. By reducing the travel industry's ecological 'footprint', companies and travellers can help the UK meet its targets for a range of international environmental treaties.

- The above information is from WWF's web site which can be found at www.wwf.org.uk

© WWF-UK

# What holiday makers really want

**responsibletravel.com urges Thomson Holidays to find out what holiday makers really want!**

The *Thomson Holidaymaker* report 2001 highlights the fact that tourists are spending more money on holidays than ever before and that they are looking for unique experiences. But it misses out on vital trends that are affecting the very core of the travel industry.

responsibletravel.com's co-founder, Justin Francis, commented: 'We congratulate Thomson Holidays on trying to find out how travellers feel, but they should really broaden their survey to include questions around travellers' concerns about social and environmental impact in destinations. Responsible travel has become a new category of travel – so it's important that the *Thomson Holidaymaker* report as well as other trend reports take this into account and add new questions to the mix'

Tearfund – one of the UK's leading overseas development charities – which published a report in January 2000, clearly indicated that tourists are more and more concerned about visiting destinations in a responsible way.

The Thomson report highlighted that meeting new people was a very important factor when deciding on a holiday destination. However, the Tearfund report went one step further by showing that 37% also felt it to be highly important that there was significant interaction with new people – who were also local to the destination.

The Tearfund report also showed that 32% of people felt it is highly important that the trip has been specifically designed to cause as little damage to the environment as possible. Meanwhile, 45% of people would be more likely to book a holiday if the tour operator had a written code to guarantee good working conditions and support for the local charities in the tourist destination.

ABTA also confirmed the Tearfund findings within industry research published in 2001, which showed that 70% of their respondents said it was important that the holidays benefited the people in the destination – via jobs and business opportunities.

---

*32% of people felt it is highly important that the trip has been specifically designed to cause as little damage to the environment as possible*

---

Graham Gordon, author of Tearfund's latest report into the tourism industry, commented: 'The Tearfund report encouraged tour operators to be more open about the impact of their activities by showing that tourists are increasingly discerning and need to see evidence that ethical policies are not just for show but are actually implemented on the ground for the benefit of local communities.'

For more information about seeing a popular tourist destination – which fulfils all your holiday needs – log onto www.responsibletravel.com, which features a variety of holidays from responsible tour operators, all of which fulfil economic, social and environmental standards – ones that help the tourists and the destinations they visit.

• The above information is from responsibletravel.com Ltd's web site which can be found at www.responsibletravel.com

© *responsibletravel.com Ltd. 2001*

# Travelling to a fairer world

## Can tourism help combat global poverty?

### Tourism: the problem and the potential

#### The tourism boom

Since the 1950s, the number of tourists travelling internationally has increased 25 fold, from 25 million to almost 600 million. In fact, according to a report published by the World Tourism Organisation, by the year 2015 there will be 1.3 billion people globetrotting, spending nearly 2 trillion US dollars (*Tourism 2020 Vision: A New Forecast*, WTO, 1997). Tourism will be the world's largest industry earning more than the oil industry or the arms trade.

But what effect will this travel boom have on developing countries?

#### The tourism problem

The rapid development of tourism can devastate local communities and environments. We've all heard people talk about their latest holiday 'find', but they warn 'get there before it's spoilt'. And many of us have experienced that sense of loss when somewhere we loved for being 'idyllic' has become commercialised or a concrete jungle. The fear is that the process will happen much quicker when nearly three times the number of people are travelling around the world!

The massive growth of tourism worldwide has resulted in the vertical integration of the travel industry where large multi-national corporations, owning their own travel agencies and airlines, can make significant savings (and profits). A two-week package holiday to India now costs half the price of a scheduled flight to Rome. Large tour operators must offer value for money to survive and whilst this may be great for the tourist, local people in a developing country may see as little as 10 pence out of every tourist pound (Economist Intelligence Unit 1992).

'It is crazy – we hardly benefit from tourism at all. Most of the money goes back out of the country. Even our farmers hardly benefit

*By Sue Wheat*

because so much of the food for tourists is imported,' says Adama Bah, director of Gambia Tourism Concern, a pressure group in The Gambia's main tourist area, supported by VSO volunteer, Val Smith, who works as coordinator for the group.

#### The tourism potential

Tourism has the potential to be an engine of change in the developing world. If more money spent by

> **The rapid development of tourism can devastate local communities and environments. We've all heard people talk about their latest holiday 'find', but they warn 'get there before it's spoilt'**

tourists remained with local people in holiday destinations, this would directly reduce poverty by giving people the income they need for basic health care, education and food.

INTERNATIONAL AIRPORT

THE ONLY PROBLEM WITH TOURISM IS THE TOURISTS

For tourists travelling to developing countries, their holiday can be an inspiring and fascinating insight into another world and often encourages us to take an interest in international issues. It can give us an increased understanding of the problems that cause poverty and respect for another country's culture. Both are powerful forces for increasing public support for international cooperation.

Indeed the Government's White Paper, *Eliminating World Poverty*, published last year by Clare Short, supports an internationally agreed target to halve the number of people living in poverty by 2015. If it is to be successful, many of the measures in it will rely on increased understanding and action from the UK public. With 20 million tourists leaving the UK each year, tourism could be a powerful catalyst for this change.

### VSO and tourism

Tourism has the potential to either help or harm the lives of some of the world's poorest people, and many of VSO's partners believe it to be the biggest challenge facing them. If tourism is to bring real benefits in the future then the voices of local people need to be heard now.

Over 1,950 VSO volunteers live and work as part of a local community and they see the effects of tourism first hand. They know the industry is changing the lives of many of the people they work with – sometimes for the better, sometimes not.

Catherine Logie, a VSO English teacher in Tana Toraja, Indonesia, said: 'We discuss development issues as they relate to Toraja, including tourism. I have taught a course called "cross-cultural understanding" in which students relate what they learn to their own experiences with tourists. I am also frequently asked for help in writing application letters in English for hotel work.'

Many communities VSO works with have felt the sharp end of tourism and are desperate for change. Volunteers report that losing land, water and access to public places are common complaints, and tourism has very clearly been associated with serious social abuses such as child sex tourism and the eviction of people from their land.

### Tourism in 2015: travelling to a fairer world – how it could work

If we make the right changes now tourism could help countries develop and communities rise out of poverty. Ideally tourists will enjoy their holidays more, locals and national economies will benefit more from tourism, and foreign tourism companies will be able to offer better holidays to their customers.

*In 2015*

Local businesses are more tightly woven into the tourism industry. Hotels will buy local produce, more local people are trained and employed in management positions.

*In 2015*

Working with the tourism industry, governments in developing countries

---

### Getting a boost from tourism

After I left school, I was a garden boy for two years, earning just Z$100 a month. As a sculptor, I am making between Z$4,000 and Z$5,000 in the same time. Now I am happy because I am working for myself. My school friends are at home without jobs. Their lives are tough, they only earn once a year after harvest time when they sell their crops. They can't support their families, but I can. When I go home, I take money, as well as essentials like sugar, flour, oil and soap. When I was a garden boy, I couldn't take them one cent.

Admire Makuvise, a sculptor at Nyanga Crafts Village, Zimbabwe

---

### How it's happening already: making the links

In St Lucia, Sunshine Harvest Fruit and Vegetable Farmers' Co-operative, consisting of 66 farmers, co-ordinates production and marketing to ensure regular supplies to hotels.

The Government and the private sector are agreeing to the need for a co-ordinated strategy. In 1994, the St Lucia Hotel Association and the Ministry of Agriculture launched an 'adopt a farmer' pilot scheme, in which hoteliers buy produce from a specified farmer at a contract price agreed before planting. Smallholders are being encouraged to produce a wide range of fruit and vegetables instead of just bananas, which in the past have been imported from the US. Loans from local banks are available to farmers at favourable rates to allow them to buy seeds and fertilisers. The potential for retaining more revenue in the island is greatly improved.

will have developed clear strategies for tourism. More money stays in the community so less people will be living in poverty.

*In 2015*

Community tourism initiatives can get credit from government financial institutions or independent credit institutions. As they are also given support from governments, industry and development agencies to help them market themselves, both at the destination and internationally, tourists and communities benefit.

*In 2015*

Environmental standards have been devised, adopted and enforced by local and national governments for foreign and local hotels. Hotels now extend water, sewage and energy facilities to local communities.

*In 2015*

Tour operators offer a better 'tourism product' through being connected to community-tourism initiatives.

Tourists are happier because their holiday experience is more culturally realistic and more beneficial to the people involved. Many have changed the way they dress and behave on holiday as well as their expectations of a holiday in a developing country.

### In 2015
Tourists will have more opportunity to buy locally produced goods and to experience local culture.

### Tour operators
Give your customers more information about the people and the places they will be visiting in your brochures, including advice on how they can visit locally owned facilities and resorts.

Develop a policy for your business on how the holidays you provide could be of more benefit to people living in the destinations you visit.

### Hotels
Start buying more goods and services locally and reducing imports. Start an environmental management programme within the hotel.

### UK Government
The Department for International Development should recognise the contribution international tourism can make in promoting development awareness among the UK public, and look into ways tourism can be used to achieve this objective.

The Department for International Development should consider the potential of international tourism to alleviate global poverty and contribute to achieving progress towards the DAC (Development Assistance Committee) targets outlined in the recent White Paper.

- This report has been written by Sue Wheat, a journalist specialising in tourism and its impacts, and a member of Tourism Concern. Contact Tourism Concern on Tel: 020 7753 3330 or e-mail them at info@tourismconcern.org.uk

- The above information is from Voluntary Service Overseas' (VSO) web site which can be found at www.vso.org.uk

# ASTA's ten commandments on eco-tourism

**W**hether you're travelling on business, pleasure or a bit of both, all the citizens of the world, current and future, would be grateful if you would respect ASTA's Ten Commandments of World Travel:

1  Respect the frailty of the earth. Realise that unless all are willing to help in its preservation, unique and beautiful destinations may not be here for future generations to enjoy.
2  Leave only footprints. Take only photographs. No graffiti! No litter! Do not take away 'souvenirs' from historical sites and natural areas.
3  To make your travels more meaningful, educate yourself about the geography, customs, manners and cultures of the region you visit. Take time to listen to the people. Encourage local conservation efforts.
4  Respect the privacy and dignity of others. Inquire before photographing people.
5  Do not buy products made from endangered plants or animals, such as ivory, tortoise shell, animal skins, and feathers.
6  Always follow designated trails. Do not disturb animals, plants or their natural habitats.
7  Learn about and support conservation-oriented programs and organisations working to preserve the environment.
8  Whenever possible, walk or use environmentally-sound methods of transportation. Encourage drivers of public vehicles to stop engines when parked.
9  Patronize those hotels, airlines, resorts, cruise lines, tour operators and suppliers who advance energy and environmental conservation; water and air quality; recycling; safe management of waste and toxic materials; noise abatement; community involvement; and which provide experienced, well-trained staff dedicated to strong principles of conservation.
10  Encourage organisations to subscribe to environmental guidelines. ASTA urges organisations to adopt their own environmental codes to cover special sites and ecosystems.

Travel is a natural right of all people and is a crucial ingredient of world peace and understanding. With that right comes responsibilities. ASTA encourages the growth of peaceful tourism and environmentally responsible travel.

- The above information is from American Society of Travel Agents' web site which can be found at www.astanet.com

# ADDITIONAL RESOURCES

You might like to contact the following organisations for further information. Due to the increasing cost of postage, many organisations cannot respond to enquiries unless they receive a stamped, addressed envelope.

**Association of British Travel Agents (ABTA)**
68-71 Newman Street
London, W1T 3AH
Tel: 020 7637 2444
Fax: 020 7637 0713
E-mail: abta@abta.co.uk
Web site: www.abta.com
ABTA is the UK's Premier Trade Association for Tour Operators and Travel Agents. ABTA's 800 tour operators and 6700 travel agency offices are responsible for the sale of some 80% of UK-sold holidays.

**Department for International Development (DFID)**
1 Palace Street
London, SW1E 5HE
Tel: 020 7023 0000
Fax: 020 7917 0019
E-mail: enquiry@dfid.gov.uk
Web site: www.dfid.gov.uk
DFID is a UK Government department, working to promote sustainable development and eliminate world poverty.

**Friends of the Earth (FOE)**
26-28 Underwood Street
London, N1 7JQ
Tel: 020 7490 1555
Fax: 020 7490 0881
E-mail: info@foe.co.uk
Web site: www.foe.co.uk
As an independent environmental group, Friends of the Earth publishes a comprehensive range of leaflets, books and in-depth briefings and reports.

**International Institute for Environment and Development (IIED)**
3 Endsleigh Street
London, WC1H 0DD
Tel: 020 7388 2117
Fax: 020 7388 2826
E-mail: mailbox@iied.org
Web site: www.iied.org
IIED is a non-profit organisation promoting sustainable patterns of world development through collaborative research, policy studies and knowledge dissemination.

**People & the Planet**
Suite 112, Spitfire Studios
63-71 Collier Street
London, N1 9BE
Tel: 020 7713 8108
Fax: 020 7713 8109
E-mail: planet21@totalise.co.uk
Web site: www.peopleandplanet.net
peopleandplanet.net provides a global review and internet gateway into the issues of population, poverty, health, consumption and the environment. It is published by Planet 21, an independent non-profit company.

**Tearfund**
100 Church Road
Teddington, TW11 8QE
Tel: 020 8977 9144
Fax: 020 8943 3594
E-mail: enquiries@tearfund.org
Web site: www.tearfund.org
Tearfund is one of the UK's leading relief and development agencies, working in partnership with Christian agencies and churches around the world to tackle the causes and effects of poverty.

**The International Ecotourism Society (TIES)**
PO Box 668
Burlington VT 05402, USA
Tel: + 1 802 651 9818
Fax: + 1 802 651 9819
E-mail: ecomail@ecotourism.org
Web site: www.ecotourism.org
The Ecotourism Society was founded in 1990 to foster a true sense of synergy between outdoor travel entrepreneurs, researchers and conservationists.

**Tourism Concern**
Stapleton House
277-281 Holloway Road
London, N7 8HN
Tel: 020 7753 3330
Fax: 020 7753 3331
E-mail: info@tourismconcern.org.uk
Web site: www.tourismconcern.org.uk
Tourism Concern is a membership organisation campaigning for ethical and fairly traded tourism.

**United Nations Environmental Programme (UNEP)**
C.P. 356, 1219 Châtelaine
Geneva, Switzerland
Tel: + 41 22 9799242
Fax: + 41 22 797 3464
E-mail: eisinfo@unep.org
Web site: www.unep.org
UNEP works to provide leadership and encourage partnership in caring for the environment.

**Voluntary Service Overseas (VSO)**
371 Putney Bridge Road
London, SW15 2PN
Tel: 020 8780 7200
Fax: 020 8780 1326
E-mail: enquiries@vso.org.uk
Web site: www.vso.org.uk
VSO is an international development charity that works through volunteers. VSO sends people, not money.

**World Tourism Organization (WTO)**
Capitán Haya, 42
28020 Madrid, Spain
Tel: + 34 91 567 81 00
Fax: + 34 91 571 37 33
E-mail: infoshop@world-tourism.org
Web site: www.world-tourism.org
The WTO is the leading international organisation in the field of travel and tourism.

**WWF-International**
Avenue Mont Blanc
CH-1196 Gland, Switzerland
Tel: + 41 22 364 91 11
Fax: + 41 22 364 53 58
Web site: www.panda.org
Promotes the wise use of the world's natural resources.

**WWF-UK**
Panda House, Weyside Park
Catteshall Lane, Godalming
Surrey, GU7 1XR
Tel: 01483 426444
Fax: 01483 426409
Web site: www.wwf.org.uk
WWF-UK is the British arm of the largest independent international conservation organisation in the world.

# INDEX